A Daughter of Leeds

Gloria Yates

Yorkshire Art Circus

in association with

Micropress

Published by: Yorkshire Art Circus
                     School Lane, Glasshoughton, Castleford, WF10 4QH, UK
                     01977-550401 e-mail admin@artcircus.demon.co.uk
and

                     Micropress
                     29 Brittainy Street
                     Petrie, Queensland 4502, Australia

Cover Design: Paul Miller of Ergo Design

Editor: Brian Lewis
Production Team: Ian Daley, Lorna Hey, Harry Malkin
Printing: FM Repro, Liversedge

ISBN: 1 898311 34 X

Classification: Autobiography

Special thanks go to Leeds Central Library for permission to use a collection of their
photographs.

Yorkshire Art Circus is a unique book publisher. We work to increase access to writing and
publishing and to develop new models of practice for arts in the community. Please write
to us for details of our full programme of workshops and our current book list.
Please look in on the Yorkshire Art Circus Web site: www.artcircus.demon.co.uk
Yorkshire Art Circus is a registered charity No 1007443.

Yorkshire Art Circus is supported by:

  City of Wakefield Metropolitan District Council Leisure Services

Foreword

In 1995 a letter from Australia arrived at the Yorkshire Art Circus accompanying a synopsis and some sample chapters of a life story. The letter ended abruptly with a dash and the line: 'and if you aren't interested now you never will be.'

We were, and two years and a lot of e-mail later, we present to you that life story alongside the poem. Yorkshire Art Circus does not usually publish poetry. We have published *In Praise of the Councillors and Aldermen of Leeds* at the beginning of Gloria's story because its subtext is about the need to use public money to provide amenities which we all can use; it shows how the political becomes the personal.

That is not the only way in which this book breaks new ground for us. This is our first international partnership. *A Daughter Of Leeds* is published jointly by Yorkshire Art Circus and by Micropress of Queensland, Australia. It is our first major publishing project using the internet.

The photographs did not travel as far as the text. Most of them come from the Leeds City Library collection, and they follow the poem more than they follow the autobiography.

The city Gloria knew as a small girl was changing. The improvements of the first decade of the century were civic improvements - squares, major shopping streets and council buildings - whereas those of the third and fourth decade relate to housing. A lot has been written about the failure of cities after the 1914-1918 War *to create a land fit for heroes* but, through its slum clearance schemes and early council estates, Leeds managed to make a mark. Compared with the ill-considered schemes of the 1960s these estates were truly heroic.

We would like to thank all the people who contributed photographs but we are especially indebted to the City Library, first for collecting and cataloguing such an excellent picture collection, then for giving us access.

In many ways Gloria's book is in praise of free public libraries, for more than most she received education because they existed. Long may they thrive.

Brian Lewis

In Praise Of The Aldermen And Councillors Of Leeds

Now let us praise
let it be written in glory
and sung to the stars
this ordinary amazing story of
the aldermen and councillors of
the City of Leeds
who early in this God-forsaking century
before the second wreckage of the world
were selected to sit on committees:
they who ordained
that the children of the city be weighed and measured
and those much below average height and weight
be given malt molasses daily at school
and furthermore they ordered
inspection of the mouths of the children
and so appalled were they at what they found
they built a building and installed within it
dentists and dental nurses and modern equipment
yea, even unto anaesthetic gas
that no child there should suffer rotting teeth
and in addition they decreed
that the eyes of the children of the city be tested

and spectacles prescribed and given free
to those like me whose parents could not pay
for them to see.
And moreover,
aware that the women of the city, trapped in childbirth
were dying of backstreet abortions,
in the very heart of the city they opened
a birth control and a VD clinic
to those in need.
Nor did these heroes stop there.
They founded scholarships with grants for uniforms
built public libraries well lit and warm
crammed them with books bound in leather...
Of golden oak the shelves,
polished the parquet floors
  Great were their works
  Awesome their energy
  Ferocious their determination.
Talk not to me of tennis players surfers footballers.
Take your cricket and golf balls and stuff them
arse-wards.
For I am a child of a great city.

In Praise Of The Aldermen And Councillors Of Leeds

Australian, yes, but not made in Australia.
Always a daughter of Leeds
and yet I never thanked those men and women
who clothed me in the delight of poetry
gave me books and a higher education
may they rest in eternal peace
may the earth enfold them
and if there is a heaven
may they ride the silver tramlines of the city
as I rode them
with the streetlights gleaming in the rain
from the tops of double-deckers
see that shining double pathway,
parallels stretching to infinity.
(It was all silver then
in the nights of my childhood.
In the blackout
I feared no dark.)
May they play in the parks, pools, gardens of the city
as I played
for they deserve no less
and heaven could give no more.

Those councillors belonged to the Labour Party
and long did they labour
to make that city New Jerusalem.
And I say unto you:
Bugger your movie stars, your Bears and Broncos.
I'd swap them all for a single member
of Leeds City Council
who in the year of our lord nineteen thirty-two
made Leeds a city
where I, being Jewish,
was fed in school not starved in camps
where the only gas I breathed was nitrous oxide
not Zyklon B
where I was lucky
very lucky
God I was lucky
to be born.

The Tram To Briggate

I am a true daughter of Leeds, born in Leeds Infirmary, bred in the streets of Sheepscar, cared for by the City Council and schooled in its classrooms. But my parents came together from North and South.

Dad was a Cockney, born within the sound of Bow Bells and, like his father, an East Ender. They knew their history back to Cromwell's time. They'd fled from the Spanish Inquisition about three hundred years back, and Bobbie, my gran, could still speak Spanish and had some years of schooling in a convent. They belonged to the oldest, proudest Jewish congregation in Britain. They were Sephardim, nobility. When they died, they did it properly; on a deathbed, surrounded by sons and daughters, making formal farewells.

I was taught how to die properly at an early age. These things mattered to my father.

My mother's family were exactly the opposite. Given half a chance, they'd mess up any occasion by weeping and wailing. They took off for eternity by fits and starts, with strokes and in comas. No firm instructions, final blessing, last words to be remembered.

Dad's family had ancestors. Mam's family were escapees from the ghetto, a tree without roots. Yet they produced some. I was told one of his relatives had been a boxer who fought, and beat, Maurice Carpentier. Knowing nothing about boxing, I accepted my career. I had to be a fighter, I'm always fighting.

One of the Benjamins had been on board the *Victory* with Nelson, so generation after generation one of the boys was called "Hardy" - "Harty" it became by the time I was born. This meant I could never be seasick, so I never was. Nelson might have been seasick, but not me. Zaidie, my grandad, was a docker, a huge man who used to swing me round his head by one ankle. I liked this.

Whilst Grandad had to fight for work, she could always hold down a job once the babies had grown. She kept the family going, lending money to others, taking their rings as pledges.

On her deathbed she stripped the rings from her fingers, giving clear instructions to return every one to its owner. Then she looked at her hands, where only one ring remained. "Now I can die with honour," she said, and did.

Dad had two elder brothers, Mick and Alec, and two younger sisters, Sally and Hetty. Their real names were, in this order: Moses, called Mick; Zachariah, called Alec; Isaac, called Jim - my Dad, in the middle - Esther who became Hetty and

Sarah who was Sally. They were not trying to hide their Jewish identities. The sheer idiocy of addressing a baby as Moses or Zachariah wore them down.

All Dad's family were good-looking. Sally was tall and dark, leggy and wide-mouthed. Hetty was delicately pretty, fragile-faced. Alec was a dead ringer for Errol Flynn. Dad wasn't too strong and lacked Alec's height and swagger, but I always thought him handsome and see him still, in the old photos, a cockney version of Clark Gable crossed with David Niven. Zaidie was the spitting image of Stalin; the family lived in awe of him. "Honour thy father and thy mother," said the Commandment. Zaidie enforced this honouring with the steel buckle of a huge belt. A sergeant in the Boer War, he had medals to prove it. Yet the total wisdom passed on from his army service in two wars was: never be the third to light up from the same match. With the first flare of a match the sniper in the opposite trench sighted; as the second smoker lit up, he aimed, and the third got the bullet.

Anyway, Dad grew up and went to school; his stamping ground was the Mile End Road which runs through the East End like an artery of history and rebellion. Pubs stood there in their scores; boozing was tribal and ritual. The family that prays together stays together, say the Catholics. My family went off to the pub and got drunk together. Beer was a liquid but effective form of social cement.

Seventy-five Ely Terrace, Stepney Green, London E1. That was where Dad's family lived. The Germans bombed it flat, and the streets around it. After the war it was just a plateau strewn with rubble where a thousand families had lived. I saw what was left with stupefaction.

Dad never got any kind of instruction in the Jewish religion. Neither did any of his brothers and sisters. They couldn't speak, read or write Hebrew. They didn't want to. None of them had the slightest idea of what it was all about. They had a jolly good time at Christmas, turkey with trimmings, pudding packed with silver threepenny bits, holly and mistletoe. If I ask myself what being Jewish had to do with them, I'm at a complete dead end. They were Jewish, and that was that. It was as if some almighty accident had hit them on the heads at the moment of birth and said: 'This one's Jewish.'

Being Jewish was strictly a part-time proposition for Dad's family. Less than part-time, in truth. They were Jewish when they were born, married and buried. Weddings and burials were always occasions for colossal expense - East Enders were happy to get into debt for years to pay for a good wedding feast. Three hundred people danced at my Uncle Alec's wedding; I still have the family photo. I was one of the bridesmaids. Our satin dresses, poke bonnets, silver-tasselled velvet cloaks, must have cost a small fortune. That was only normal. The idea of a quiet wedding would have seemed like a sick joke to them.

However, marrying out was no joke. The family threat was awesome and complete. "If you ever marry out, you'll be dead to us." Not disinherited or disowned: dead. Nobody would ever speak to you or about you as long as you lived. You'd be dead before you were buried. They'd read the funeral service over you, and that was that. The end.

Tribal and proud, this was Dad's community. They were proud of being Jewish, proud of being English, proudest of all as East Enders. They wouldn't have changed places with anyone. They lived in a free country, in the city of London. Stepney Green was the fields of paradise to them, no less. When Wordsworth looked upon the sleeping heart of London, he said, "Earth hath not anything to show more fair." Well, that was how Dad's family felt about Petticoat Lane on a Sunday morning. Who could wish for anything more?

*

My father's side of the family had an immense capacity for enjoying life. My mother's - an immense capacity for suffering. And why not? They had not enjoyed three hundred years of safety in England. They'd fled from pogroms in Latvia, Lithuania and the Ukraine. Wave after wave of pogroms caused wave after wave of Jewish migration. They were refugees, they were desperate, they sold everything they had to escape. They landed at Hull, but couldn't afford tickets to Manchester or the dream ticket to America. Still, they went as far as they could. The idea was to put as many miles as possible between your family and the Latts, the Litvaks and the Lithuanians. Long before Hitler these people were burning Jews alive.

Mam's family couldn't afford tickets to the US. They reached Hull, were trained to Leeds, taken off the train by the rescue service and billeted on families who had a roof over their heads. From then on everyone chipped in.

Mam told me a lot about this time. When a new train load came in, Grandma put on a multi-pocketed apron. She'd go knocking from door to door, begging for the newcomers. There was no money available, but since all the families had someone

working, there was food in those houses. No matter how poor they were, people always gave something. Half a loaf of bread, a packet of tea, flour in a paper bag. She'd go back with her apron full and take it to the new family, and weeks later they'd be helping the next train-load to settle in.

That's how I got the idea that after the family, the most important thing in life is helping your neighbours. Mam had this in common with Dad. The neighbours were your friends, your salvation. In half a century I can remember only one quarrel with them, though that nearly ended in a lynching. But on the whole, there was peace, respect for the community and honour for the elders who'd organised the exodus from Europe. Many started their working lives in sweatshops owned by these same Jews. It was work - all Jews together - and they could take Saturday off instead of Sunday, keeping the Sabbath. Nothing else mattered.

Like Dad, my mother completely lacked any explanation of religion. She didn't look Jewish - she had classic Irish colouring, grey eyes, black hair and a pink complexion that never tanned. Her mouth was a true Cupid's bow and remained so to the end. "This one's Jewish," some God had decided, but explanations there were none. Being a girl, she wasn't sent to Hebrew school, but as far as I can make out, none of them were, except Max. He was last born and the only one allowed to stay at school, because he was such a sickly child, they were sure work in the sweatshops would kill him.

The whole family discussed this and there was total agreement. Max had asthma and occasional fits. So those who were working agreed to pay their share to put Max through medical school. They wanted to make a doctor of him - alas, Max wasn't bright enough. He was relegated to Dental School, a safe haven for failed medical students, and flunked his finals twice, becoming a dentist on his third attempt. Mam was the clever one, but she was taken from school at thirteen and sent "into the tailoring" though her teachers said she could win a scholarship. Education was for boys. For girls it was unnecessary, a positive evil. Girls who got educated didn't get married.

This stance against educating girls was taken by both sides of the family. Auntie Hetty, Dad's youngest sister, was also a clever girl encouraged to try for a scholarship, but she wasn't allowed. She was dragged out of school on the pretext that she was "messing around with boys"; the real reason was to ensure she didn't ruin her chances of marriage. "Getting ideas" was the danger.

LOWER HEADROW 1936

In the 1840s Leeds was well to the fore in municipal planning. Its councillors and aldermen commissioned Cuthbert Broderick to build a splendid, no expenses spared, town hall. In 1939 a later generation had cleared land in Lower Headrow and were considering improving the frontage of the Art Gallery. This is an enhanced photograph. Improvements to the Art Gallery were never carried out.

But Mam's family regarded booze as the devil itself. Mam's sister Katie had married a Jew who drank. He liked to heap up the fire to get a really good blaze going. One night he came home shicker, and she woke up to find the house on fire. She threw her babies down to the neighbours' waiting arms and jumped from the upstairs window. But she broke her back on the pavement and died in hospital. He survived.

So Mam's family loathed pubs and beer, but this had its tragi-comic side. When Uncle Gaby's beloved Valerie left him, he took to drowning his sorrows in coffee. You'd walk into any milk bar and sure enough Gaby'd be there, sitting in a corner, staring sadly into a lukewarm cup. Sometimes I wished he'd get raving drunk instead.

My mother could sing like an angel. She won prizes for singing at Jewish concerts; she sang in Yiddish and the old men wept and told Bobbie and Zaidie they were blessed with a wonderful daughter. But though a boy could become a cantor, a singing career for a girl was taboo. Mam was taken out of school at twelve and became a trousers-hand, working a fifteen-hour day in the summer. She said if they hadn't let her sing at the machine she'd have gone insane.

The big treat for working girls, the wonderful thrill of the week, was to visit the vast Lyons tea-shop in Briggate on a Saturday afternoon. You sat down at a lovely linen-covered table and you were waited on. There were carpets on the floor, candelabras on the ceiling, gilt-edged mirrors shining on the walls. For sixpence you could get a banana split on a silver salver, served with a long silver-plated spoon, brought to you by a waitress in full uniform. Going into Lyons was like entering the gates of heaven.

All the Jewish girls went there, and the Jewish boys. They sat within sight of each other, giggled and goggled and ogled, then negotiated with friends, sisters and brothers to get introduced. Thus it was that one Saturday afternoon Dad spotted Mam and found another girl willing to do the honours - she knew Mam's sisters.

He was led to her table, chatted her up and asked her out.

She claimed he didn't have the cash to pay for the meal on their first date, and she paid for both of them. He never denied this. They had a passionate courtship, mostly in Roundhay Park where courting couples went to feed the ducks on long summer evenings. The ducks prospered: they were prolific and very fat. There's a

LOWER HEADROW 1940

War had begun and sandbags protected the base of Central Library. The War Memorial had been re-located and was ready and waiting for the names of the 1939-45 dead.

photo of Mam and Dad intertwined around a tree, a very handsome couple. On one of those summer evenings I was conceived, somewhere around the Big Lake, at the end of August 1931. They were married on November 29th in the same year.

*

From the day that Mam married Dad, a miracle happened. Because of Dad, she never had to work in the factory again.

We all know the phrase, "She never forgave him for that." But this was exactly the other way around. Whatever else Dad did, he saved her from a life of sheer drudgery, of such hellish boredom that all his sins dwindled to peccadilloes against this one continuous act of salvation.

Mam and Dad began their married life at 72 Benson Street, off North Street, in Leeds 1. It was a city slum, though there were worse. The house was in a terrace and consisted of two rooms, one up and one down, with no bathroom, toilet or kitchen. A lavatory block was situated at the end of the street - the far end. Eight families shared each lavatory. Mam told me she used to go there, find someone had shat or sicked up all over the seat, go back for a bucket of water and scrub it clean. The next time she wanted to use it, there'd be another mess. But we did have running water in the downstairs room, which was more than Dad's family had in London. They were still pumping it from the yard.

Every drop of hot water had to be heated on the fire in kettles or pots and pans; that was true in both homes. But Leeds did not have the East End's palatial bath houses. Once a week you bathed in a galvanised tub in front of the fire. Cooking was done in the oven next to the coals, and kettles were boiled on the fire.

Around Benson Street the air was foul. It had a special acrid edge. Soot and acid together tainted everything. Atmospherically, Leeds was the most polluted city in England. Across the main road, North Street, was a withered stretch of land known as Sheeny Park, planted with dirty daffodils or tulips. On the far side of this floral extravaganza was a shull, a synagogue, and near that, a school: Lovell Road Mixed Infants. Dad's factory was further, but within easy walking distance. He was the best cabinet-maker they had. For being such a skilled workman he was made foreman at the princely wage of three pounds ten shillings a week

And now to explain why the pub was so much more attractive than our home. Frankly, babies stank.

QUARRY HILL FLATS

This major building project stood on slum clearance land. Built between 1935 and 1941 it housed in the region of 3,200 people.

If Hitler had conquered England this would have become his Northern headquarters. The flats were demolished between 1975 and 1978. The West Yorkshire Playhouse now stands on the site.

There were no washing machines, no dryers and no disposable nappies.

For dirty nappies there were buckets with lids. When these were full you boiled the nappies in a copper on the fire in the same room where you lived. And the room filled with clouds of steam and stank of disinfectant and shit. Then you had to dry the nappies. How?

The climate of Leeds wasn't sunny but if you had a garden, a brisk windy day dried the clothes on the line. The no-garden slum method was to string clotheslines across the street, which worked quite well for those in streets that didn't have tall double-decker buses going past at five-minute intervals. For Mam, the only way to dry clothes was a contraption that was lowered from the ceiling when you'd got a good coal fire going. On a wet day in summer this made the whole house damp and it reeked of wet washing.

On a cold day in winter it effectively cut off all the heat of the fire, which was retained by white walls of steaming nappies. It was a miracle all Sheepscar babies weren't murdered at birth. The fact that they mostly survived is witness to the strength of parental love and the desire to produce another generation. People are crazy about themselves.

Mam hated Sheepscar and longed to get out of the slums into the suburbs where the air was fit to breathe and the parks were real. She was wasting her time urging Dad to move because he'd already discovered how convenient it was for his Mecca, the Sheepscar Working Men's Club. Halfway between factory and home, it had all the attractions an East Ender could hope for: cheap booze, billiards and snooker, buxom barmaids, smoke haze. Mam learned to cook. It wasn't easy, and there were many mistakes in the early days. No matter. Dad consoled himself at the club. Mam was pregnant with me.

She was totally ignorant of how babies are born.

When I started to be born, she tried to push me back. I'm not making this up. She told me herself, said she was horrified - she didn't know where babies came out - she thought they'd operate to take it out of her stomach.

To stop her screams, they used too much ether. After I was finally born, she didn't come round. They sent a policeman to Madeloff's to fetch Dad to see her. They only did that when someone was dying. But Mam didn't die. It was 4 June 1932.

Traumatised by the long labour and the overdose of ether, she was soon violently ill with breast fever. She lay in hospital for three months, unable to feed me or even see me. As a matter of fact, she didn't even get to name me. I was sent to Bobbie who'd already brought up nine children. They put me in a crib in front of the fire, attached a stocking to the bars so they could rock it when I cried, and tried to feed me; I wouldn't take any of the milk formulas on sale. Then in desperation they gave me ordinary cow's milk. That was accepted. To this day I wouldn't rate the best wine in the world, however expensive, over a glassful of creamy milk at blood heat. I'm easy to please.

Fanny and Sadie, my aunties, chose my name. At the time Gloria Swanson was popular, and they needed something that began with a G, so Gloria it was. But of course they couldn't call a baby Gloria. I had golden hair, and the Yiddish equivalent of Gloria was Goldie or Golda. So Goldie I became for the first few years of my life, and when people were feeling affectionate I was Goldalie.

The big drama in my life was this: while I was being bathed in the zinc tub in front of the fire, and relatives came, they would always ask, "Which do you love best, your mammy or your daddy?"

There was a moment of enormous impending danger. The truth was, I loved Daddy best.

I dared not say so. I don't know how I knew this. What I had to say was, "I love them both jus' the same!"

This was always greeted with applause and laughter. Obviously it was the right thing to say. It was my first remembered sensation of danger and my first lie. Why did I love Daddy best? I've no idea. She took me out in the pram and pushed the pushchair; he hoisted me up to ride on his shoulders. She was always there to my growing awareness, he had scarcity value. He never tried to make me eat anything I didn't like; on the other hand, he never made delicious strudels or kuchen, or soothed my cuts and bruises.

Across our street was a fruit shop with nets of red pomegranates hanging outside. My friend Doreen lived next door; she had golden hair and green eyes. Her Mam was Auntie Tilly and her Dad Uncle Solly. Your friendliest neighbours were always called Auntie and Uncle. You'd have at least a dozen aunts and uncles in the street.

Mam bought a blue pushchair for me on the never-never and pushed me into town every Saturday to pay the weekly instalments. That pushchair was a godsend

when I got whooping-cough; Mam took to the tramways, hauling me and the pushchair onto the majestic trams of Route No3 to Roundhay Park.

Dad took me the other way, to Leeds Market and Pets' Alley. There in a double row of pet shops you were surrounded by singing birds, rabbits, kittens, puppies and chooks. Dad and I had exactly the same ideas about animals.

We wanted a puppy. Mam said no.

Years later I understood why. She'd watched a series of kittens get mown down by corporation buses, and she knew well that no puppy stood a chance of survival in that street. Back then I thought she was cruel. Dad and I must have egged each other on to the point where he actually bought me a puppy, but she forced him to take it back.

*

Then in December 1932, Madeloff's went on strike. All the cabinet-makers came out. Dad didn't have to strike. He was earning much higher wages than the other workers. Nevertheless he joined the men on the picket lines. It was a cold winter. Standing in the snow for hours on end did more damage to his health than all the long hours of work and the mucky air. The strike lasted six weeks and Dad got pneumonia. Worse was to come.

When the strike was over, all the men were taken back except Dad. Madeloff refused to have him. He was seen as a traitor by the bosses of every joinery in Leeds - blacklisted. He was the only foreman who'd struck with the men. The men Dad had lost his job for didn't care enough about the issue to strike for him.

For the rest of his life Dad was a political cynic.

Thank God, after a few weeks, Madeloff changed his mind and took Dad back. All through the strike and the ensuing weeks, it was Mam's family that paid the rent and brought the food. Luckily "the tailoring" had strikes that didn't coincide with the cabinet-making.

Though Dad voted Labour for the rest of his life, he learned not to depend on socialists or communists. His cynicism was cheerful, but Mam's was bitter.

"He went on strike and stood in the picket lines and left me with no food in the house and a little baby," she complained. Well, we live and learn.

FAMILY - QUARRY HILL FLATS 1939

Although the structure of the Quarry Hill Flats was ultramodern - precast cladding on a steel frame - and the insides of the rooms offered all modern amenities such as hot and cold water, a bathroom and inside loo and waterborne refuse disposal, the tenants filled the rooms with Victorian and Edwardian furnishings. The picture, which looks to be a print of a Lord Leighton reflects the elitist fine art taste of the 1880s. The glass vases were for ornament, not for flowers. The statue of Christ and the Sacred Heart suggest that this is a Roman Catholic family.

*

My longest excursion was to London; when I was three, we all went down "home" for a family Christmas. The thrill of it! The heavenly smell - crates full of tangerines wrapped in silver paper. That's when my Uncle Alec bought me a huge book of fairytales for Christmas and I convinced my doting parents that I could read.

I couldn't, of course. I just had a wonderful memory. Whenever Mam read me a story she moved her finger along the words she was reading. Putting two and two together, I realised that the spoken words were just above her moving finger. It didn't take long for me to give as fine an imitation of reading as any child ever produced. Soon a real storm was raging over my reading ability. My grandparents claimed I couldn't possibly be reading at three, my parents claimed that I could, and was.

Finally they put me to the test.

The whole family encircled me, still arguing loudly over my literary pretensions. They presented me with one of my own books open at random and demanded that I read.

Of course I read. They were all picture books and I went by the pictures.

They were baffled. They were sure I couldn't read. They tried hiding one page while I read the other, but I knew the shapes of different words and would stop on the last one on the page, even if the word was "and" or "it". They switched books on me, but I knew all my own books. Finally my grandparents admitted that I could read - what a relief! - and at this moment, someone said, "She ought to go to Oxford University!"

That was a fateful remark.

I learned that when people asked me, "What do you want to do when you grow up?" the thing to do was answer, "I'm going to go to Oxford University."

This earned cheers, jeers, rounds of applause. It was obviously a witty reply that reduced the assembled company to stitches. At the time Oxford did admit women, but only just. To get into any university a woman would have to be both very rich and exceedingly clever. The East Enders thought it amazing cheek for a little girl from the slums of Leeds to prattle of going to Oxford. As cheek, it was priceless. But to me, it was no joke. Oxford was just the name of a place, and I was

GLORIA BENJAMIN IN KINDERGARTEN

This much damaged photograph shows Gloria at her infants' school. The Lord Mayor and Lady Mayoress are making a visit but no one seems to remember why.
Very few working class families had a camera in the 1930s and there are few pictures of interiors of homes. Working class people appeared accidentally on press shots - like Gloria at Infants School here - or on seaside promenades.

going there. I'd made up my mind. I didn't think going to university would entail any effort on my part; when I went to the Zoo, I was taken there, just as I'd been taken on the train to London. Oxford from then on became my destination.

*

Returning to Leeds, I was introduced to the joys of kindergarten. It was delightful. My teacher there was called Miss Mouse, believe it or not, and I adored her. That's all I can remember about Miss Mouse, but it is enough: Kids of my age, wearing, among other articles, a clean white handkerchief proudly pinned to my jersey. I'd lost all my baby fat and turned into a rather skinny kid with straight hair, a fringe, and big brown eyes. The kindergarten was the first place where I met and played with little boys. Little girls I knew from my cousins and Doreen-across-the-road. Little boys were strange kittle-kattle who played with trains and occasionally fought with me.

There was a wonderful range of toys to play with, far more than any parents could afford. But the best toy of all, as I remember, was handmade. I've never seen anything like it before or since. It was an entire hat shop.

Not real hats, of course, just big enough to fit your thumb or finger. Each one was a different style and colour, a miniature lady's hat, a dream of a hat. There must have been over a hundred hats in the little hat shop and I played with them by the hour. I should have ended up with a hat complex, or at least a desire to own a dozen hats, or failing that - an interest in fashion. No way. I own one battered hat today, and wear it to keep off the sun. The sweet delight of that little hat shop was complete in itself - God bless the woman who made it.

I think I was four when formal education started at Lovell Road School across Sheeny Park. Once again I was happy to leave the confines of Benson Street. When I asked, "Why?" and Mam couldn't answer, she'd say, "Because Y is a crooked letter." All my life I've read horror stories about the awful experiences of slum kids at school. Bullshit, crap, lies. I loved it.

Mam was furious. She complained that I started to smile the moment I walked through the school gates. Well, why shouldn't I?

School was logical, it was organised - home wasn't. They told you clearly what you ought to do; they didn't suddenly hit you halfway across the room for

OPENING OF AN ELECTRIC TRAMWAY 1910

By the 1930s the tramway system was no longer expanding. New routes were being served by buses. Gloria was in the last generation to experience romantic tram rides.

nothing. At home, I'd pick up the scissors on Friday night, intending to cut out some pictures, an action perfectly acceptable on any other night. Suddenly a clout would slam me against the wall. What for? Why? Why was Friday night different from any other night? I was being smacked for sins against the Sabbath when I didn't even know the days of the week. Even when I learned which days were Friday and Saturday, why couldn't I cut or write or draw on these days? They'd taught me to do these things themselves and practically cheered me for doing them. Don't think I saw my parents as religious; they were simply unpredictable lunatics, because the religious part was never explained to me. Every Friday night she lit the Shabbas candles and said something in Yiddish, and then if I played with the dripping wax - candle wax is lovely stuff to play with - she'd go crazy. She was not reliable the way the teachers at school were reliable. There were other things wrong with my parents: he started to push me away whenever he sat in his big armchair and I went to kiss and crawl all over him.

"You're too big for that now," they would say - especially Mam, who was jealous, though I don't know how I knew. "You're a big girl now."

Typical of their unaccountable antics were the carryings-on at Pesach - Passover. Suddenly she'd stand on a chair to reach a cupboard high up the wall, never used normally. She'd take down a load of dusty china, untouched since the year before. Then the zinc bath - my bath - was dragged out, balanced between two chairs and filled with sudsy hot water. The "Pesadicky" china was reverently washed. After that we had no bread for ten days, but lived on matzos and sponge cake, with special treats galore. What did it all mean? Years later I realised she got so mad when I asked "Why?" because she didn't know the answer herself. She cooked special dishes for Pesach because her family had always cooked those dishes at that time. What the feast was about I had to find out years later.

Mam and Dad were still arguing over moving out of the slums. Mum's parents were now in Harehills, on the hills breathing clean air, while we were still in the Aire valley, where smog lingered from scores of factory chimneys. Dad had dug himself in and refused to move, though he could well afford it. Mam wanted a rented house in Harehills, but he'd already got what he wanted. The Jewish community had built another mecca named the Jubilee Hall, five minutes from Sheepscar Working Men's Club and both of them close to Madeloff's. Why ruin his lifestyle?

*

Your parents couldn't visit you in Killingbeck Isolation Hospital. And there I was, lonely, ill and isolated with diphtheria and jaundice - today they call it hepatitis.

My Mam and Dad sent comics and fairytale books. There was some argument over whether these should be given to me, as they thought that a child of five couldn't read, and if she could, she shouldn't. However, in the end, they handed them over. By this time I'd learned to read. One day everything I'd learned by heart popped into place, linked itself to the printed words I'd been following on the pages, and it all made sense.

There were some adverts at the back of the fairytale book and this was the one I remember today: it showed a group of cheering children sitting round a table and underneath a verse:

Bread and milk at a party?
Oh no! The children cried
But the milk was Nestle's milk
Spread nice and thick and creamy on slices of bread!
Hooray! The children cried
For Nestle's milk!

My mother sent her best-baked cake and biscuits to the hospital. The nurses self-righteously pointed out that everything had to be shared with all the others in the ward. I got exactly one biscuit. Nobody else's Mam seemed to send anything, so I resented this enforced altruism. I thought I should get all the cake and biscuits.

Mam and Dad sent a doll; this got smashed in the post. The nurses told me that the doll had been sent and was smashed, which made me feel worse than if they'd said nothing. Maybe that was the intention. They wouldn't even let me see the smashed doll until I was almost leaving. That was about the only doll I ever had bought for me, which raises the question: What were my parents playing at? They always behaved as if nothing was further from their minds than producing educated offspring, yet I remember plenty of picture books and never a doll.

There aged five I made a discovery about myself. I have no visual memory. I

couldn't remember what Mam and Dad looked like. In my mind, I was very frightened. I searched hour after hour for the memory of their faces. There was nothing.

Half a century. I still can't remember people's faces if I try to recall them as faces but now I have a handy trick: I can often snatch a quick picture if I try to recall them moving, performing some familiar action. But in those days, at the Fever Hospital, I was scared stiff. Still, I knew who I was.

I was Goldie Gloria Benjamin of 72 Benson Street, off North Street, Leeds 1. I was Freda Benjamin's little girl. I was Jimmy Benjamin's little girl. My problem was, how would they ever know me? I assumed that everybody had the same problem. If I couldn't remember them, how would they remember me?

I learned enough about the routine of being discharged from Killingbeck to worry me. When you were well enough to go home, they came with your real clothes and dressed you. But there was never only one child to go - a group of half a dozen would be put in an ambulance and driven to the hospital gates, about half a mile away.

Outside the gates, a group of parents would be waiting.

What happened then? Who would know who was whose?

Would I ever find my parents again?

Well, I worked this one out by logic. Since children were given back to their parents every week, my problem must be quite common. No doubt the grownups had organised something; in fact they must have arranged for Someone. This Someone would be an Introducer.

The Introducer would ride with us in the ambulance to the gates, and it would be her job to say: "Mrs Benjamin, this is your daughter Goldie. Goldie Benjamin, this is your mother, Freda Benjamin." And so on.

Even from the beginning I knew how to invent things to help me figure out the world.

Eventually the glad moment came. I was going home. A nurse came with my very own clothes and dressed me as if I were a baby. While she dressed me, I stood on the bed. Standing up felt queer. When she finished, I jumped off the bed. It was just an ordinary jump, the bed was the right height for jumping, but I fell flat on my face. I'd been lying down for six weeks. I'd forgotten how to walk.

Before I had time to worry over this I was bundled into the going-home

CIVIC HALL 1933

Designed by E Vincent Harris and opened by King George V and Queen Mary in August 1933, the Civic Hall was built during a time of economic depression; 90% of the workforce were taken from the unemployment register.

ambulance with the others who'd served their sentence. Within three minutes we were at the gates and there I found, to my immense everlasting relief, that I didn't need any Introducer. The moment I set eyes on Mam and Dad, I knew. They were standing together with a blue pushchair, having been warned that my legs were too weak for walking.

So we met again and with much rejoicing, went home.

*

Our new house was in Harehills; we actually had a bath and bathroom - but no hot water - and an indoor toilet of our very own. There were two bedrooms - not one - I had a whole bedroom to myself. No buses roared past the doors - and there were two doors, a front and a back. We also had two gardens, a pocket-handkerchief of a garden at the front, and an apron-sized garden at the back, where there was, luxury of luxuries, a clothesline and a clothes prop, and our own dustbin, and some grass. There were two rooms downstairs - not one - and in the kitchen, set up ready and waiting for me, was my coming-home present.

Made of lovely golden wood, handmade by my own Dad, with a chair of golden wood to match, it stood there: Goldie's desk. Glowing with pride and happiness, I sat down at my new desk without a word. There was nothing more I wanted in the whole world.

In those days Harehills was a highly respectable working-class suburb, where housewives scar-stoned their back steps and were proud to hang out the washing all radiant with Persil and Rinso. Our house, 8 Hares Terrace, Leeds 8 - still my house really, though I live in Queensland and look out of the window at a swimming pool and palm trees - was a firm little piece of the universe, stable as Everest, fixed as the Taj Mahal. Three minutes away, no more, was Potty Park. Potternewton Park was its real name. It had bowling greens, tennis courts, rose gardens and a mansion at the top of a hill. Though many lawns were marked *KEEP OFF THE GRASS* and defended stoutly by a park keeper with peaked hat and spiked stick, there were lots of benches where you might sit, sheds to shelter from the rain and even places where kids were allowed to play. There was a huge grey granite stone called Speakers Stone. Loony men used to stand on this stone and rave on about politics. Nobody listened; this was democracy.

I have said I had everything I wanted. Alas, grownups will not leave kids alone to enjoy life in its perfection. Relatives and friends kept asking me if I wouldn't like a little brother or sister to play with?

No, I would not.

I had plenty of kids of my own age to play with. I had Adam and Ivy across the road. Adam was my boyfriend. We'd been born in the same ward, in the same hospital, Leeds Infirmary, and our mothers had been next-bed to each other. Six hours separated us.

Adam got lots of comics but couldn't read. For the price of reading him his own comics, I was permitted to bully them both. We played schools by the hour.

Naturally a teacher needs more than just two in her class. I had additional pupils: Raymond Baker, Raymond Fiddler and Roy Watson, plus a Michael who must have been my real object of desire. Whenever we played doctors and patients in his garden shed, I was the doctor and he was always the patient. He'd lie down to be examined with great alacrity - and that's all I can remember! Except that this game was immensely satisfactory. Nothing else.

Adam from across the road had a glamorous mother. I used to wish my mother looked like her; she wore high heels, pretty clothes, dyed her hair red and walked swinging her hips. She was in fact the only freelance Jewish prostitute in Leeds. I knew her as Auntie Millie and did not realise her rarity value or the fact that she was a prostitute. But I knew that Adam and Ivy would come home from school hungry to find themselves locked out of their own house, so Mam fed them on bread and jam. Sometimes she complained bitterly about this and I used to think she was mean. I was wrong; she couldn't bear to see the kids go hungry - but Millie was earning a mint.

Just as I'd loved Lovell Road Infants School, I took to my new school: Cowper Street Elementary. Whoever ran Leeds Education Committee, God bless them. The teachers were kind and devoted, the methods about half a century ahead of the rest of the world. For instance, we did arithmetic in groups sitting at different tables. There was no hurry and no pressure; as soon as I'd finished all the sums on one card, I'd trot along to the wall where there'd be the next lot waiting, hanging in pockets marked Group A.

And home?

In that precious year between five and six, before my first sister was born, I reigned like a queen. All eldest children are only children too just so long as they have no competition, and it didn't occur to me that my sensible parents would ever want more than they had already. I was satisfied with them, why shouldn't they be satisfied with me? Little did I suspect their treachery. All this nonsense about "Wouldn't you like a little playmate?" had some very nasty foundations. Even though I pointed out time after time that I'd plenty of kids my own age to play with, my parents had plotted together and after three months of moving to the new house, Mam was pregnant.

Mind you, before Betty came, life was not unalloyed happiness. Mam's parents became ill and whenever we went to the big house in Harehills Terrace, the talk would be of Hitler and the threat of war. My Bobbie, bless her heart, used to save the biggest bananas for me. She bought them from a man who came round with a horse and cart selling Fyffe's bananas. My Zaidie, a kind white-haired old man, who worked a Hoffman's presser in a tailoring factory, used to save his Woodbine cigarette cards for me.

My uncle Gaby would play "shops" with me by the hour, but as I scuttled back and forth, selling cigarette cards to one only to get more given by the other, I would hear about Mussolini and Franco, Germany building its army, Stalin standing up to Hitler. The year Betty was born was 1938. I had the vaguest possible notion of war, but everybody talked about it. War to me meant fighting, and the only fighting I'd seen was angry children hitting each other. When the grownups went on about war, I imagined an immense playground full of angry children hitting each other with no bell to ring to bring them back to the classroom. Any modern child of five has seen more horrors on television than I saw in my whole childhood, more's the pity.

Nevertheless there must have been an edge of horror to the Saturday family conversations. All over Europe Jews who'd fled from one wave of pogroms to countries like France and Britain were realising their own danger, yet in Leeds, by a weird irony of fate, I, who would have been herded into a concentration camp and starved to death had I lived in Germany, was weighed and measured and deemed to be in need of extra nourishment!

Stalwarts of progress, the City of Leeds Education Committee knew that they had thousands of undernourished, undersized kids growing up in their city, and they were determined to do something about it. Every playtime out came a huge jar

TEMPLAR STREET 1931

Leeds was the centre of the cheap clothing industry. In a circle around the centre were districts of small sewing sweatshops.

of a sweet sticky heavenly substance we used to call malt. This could be bought in chemists' shops under the trade name of "Virol"; it was actually a mixture of thick treacle and cod-liver oil, the latter included to prevent rickets. The taste of the treacle drowned out the cod-liver oil so effectively that we all loved it. At the cry of, "Line up for your malt!" out came the jar and a very large tablespoon. We all shared the same spoon, licking it shining clean without complaint.

How can I ever say thank you to those men and women who cared so much for the children of Leeds? How can I get through to a different generation whose heroes are pop singers and sports stars, that these people who made sure that hungry children got free milk and malt, these are the real heroes? I did not even thank them myself when I grew up. Yet now when I remember, "Let us all praise famous men and our fathers that begat us", praise the councillors of the City of Leeds.

May their names be blessed for evermore.

*

In October 1937 Mosley, the leader of the British blackshirts, declared a march on the East End of London. Rightly perceiving that this was the heartland of British Jewry he decided to take himself and his Fascist thugs down the Mile End Road.

The Establishment decreed that Mosley had the right of free speech. His march upon the Mile End would be protected by mounted police.

The East Enders sent out the word; *They shall not pass.*

They barricaded the Mile End Road.

It sounds so easy. But that barricade was a man-made miracle and until you know the East End, you can't understand what they achieved.

Of all the roads in London, it was the widest, and they had nothing to use for the barricade. In those days poor people did not have cars or vans. They used prams and pushchairs and kitchen furniture. They dragged out beds and cots and mattresses, armed themselves with sticks, kettles, pots and pans. Mosley came marching flanked by mounted police, and the East End rose in their thousands and blocked his way. He was stopped, as they had promised. His power was broken on the Mile End Road.

Because he was stopped by ordinary people using pans and pushchairs,

Cockney jeers against mounted police, he became the laughing-stock of England. The tale of his defeat created echoes that lasted all through my childhood. What I learned from the oft-repeated tale was this:

Stop them while you can. Fight as soon as you can. Never wait; while you're waiting, they are gathering strength. Don't be brave and suffer in silence, that way leads to the concentration camps. Scream when you're hurt, hit out and bash, you'll live longer.

I took the tale personally because I was too young to take it any other way. It was my blueprint for behaviour, my model for life. Fight meant survive.

*

A brief note on romance. For at least ten years of my life, from five to fifteen, I was convinced I was going to marry Adam-across-the-road and have twelve children, six boys and six girls. Though bitterly opposed to having a little brother or sister "to play with", the one objection I could see to twelve of my own was that twenty-four would be even better. Occasionally I veered to twenty-four and the only reason I settled for twelve was I couldn't decide on names for twenty-four. The first boy would be David, the first girl Rosalind. Then came Alan and Alanna, and after them, a blank.

Nor did I think it demeaning to marry Adam Barratt, who couldn't read his own comics. I was no intellectual snob. As Adam grew up, he proved to be a skilled and daring fighter, a boy who had his own gang and who walked on the spikes of the schoolyard railings. When his Mam sent him to bed at six o'clock on a glorious summer evening, she took the precaution of locking him in. Oh the problems of living in a private brothel. Adam shinned down the drainpipe to roam the streets and climbed back up again when he was ready for bed.

When we were six, Adam and I fell in love.

We couldn't help it. We knew we were created for each other. The stars in their courses had arranged our love and eventual marriage. The twelve children were a matter of choice - my choice. Adam said I could have as many as I liked, and I thought this very generous of him.

Our parents encouraged us, rightly so, since Adam lived exactly opposite, we strung a piece of string across the road linking our bedroom windows, and sent messages by matchboxes on the 'wire'. We were close enough to have shouted the messages (love you xxxx) but it was more romantic to send them by matchbox. Some streets nearby weren't exactly unsafe but there were rival gangs, so as I grew up Adam was often sent to accompany me on errands, with specific orders to protect me. This satisfied both of us.

One summer's day when I was six or seven, we were in Potty Park with my Mam. Adam was worried. The time had come for him to propose and he knew it. He was never backward in coming forward.

"Will you marry me?" he asked.

"Yes, but you'll have to ask my mother," I told him.

"Alright then."

He took my hand. I remember this as the most thrilling moment.

"Mrs Benjamin," he said firmly, "I want to marry your daughter Gloria."

Mam did not laugh.

"I don't mind, but you'll have to wait till she grows up."

That settled it. I was engaged, my troth was plighted, and no Juliet could have loved her Romeo more than I loved Adam-across-the-road.

Ah sweet mystery of life, at last I've found thee.

Oh at last I know the meaning of it all -

Don't think I'm joking. Adam wanted to marry me, and that changed my life. Because I knew I was going to marry him and have twelve children, my mind was free to dream of Oxford, adventures, writing great books, making long impossible journeys. I didn't have to worry about pleasing other boys, make-up, seductive trickery of all kinds. Always at the core of my self there was this sweet certainty of being loved. I could say No, and I did, time and time again, to the almost-right suitors smiled on by parents and neighbours, the respectable wrong ones that I'd have torn myself apart trying to live with.

I didn't marry him. I've never had any children.

I was forty-five before I found the man who fitted my arms as no other man has ever done. But I'm still in love with Adam. He is here, in my mind, something more than a memory. There's a place where we are always together. We are only six or seven, and Mam is sitting on the grass, waiting to hear what Adam has to say. She can tell from his face that it is something very serious.

And it is.

THE BAILEY LOCKHART BUILDING

Not all the clothing manufacturers were small businesses. At the top of North Street, close to Gloria's house, was this major "mantle" manufacturer seen here. This photograph was taken in 1930.

*

Into each life some rain must fall. Rain brings new life but it's a dreary nuisance when falling. My parents' attempts to prepare me for the coming birth began and ended with pressure to accept a little playmate. But I was no fool. I could see with my own eyes what happened when one of these playmates arrived. Alan was lumbered with Ivy, forced to drag her everywhere, made responsible for her safety. What use was a four-year-old girl to a seven-year-old boy? If Mam and Dad had talked to me at length and explained that they wouldn't be around forever, that brothers and sisters were better than your ordinary little playmate, I might have accepted Betty's birth with less pain.

As it was, my resistance to their offer caught them off balance. They simply back-pedalled and Mam refused to admit she was pregnant. A cousin called Ken, red-haired and handsome, arrived on a visit to Alan and Ivy. Being older - perhaps even as old as ten - he was stronger than Alan and more knowledgeable. He'd automatically taken over leadership of our gang.

Once, looking at a cat slinking heavily along, he announced:

"That cat's pregnant. Like your Mam."

I was indignant. "My Mam's not pregnant!"

"Yes she is. You can always tell. They get fat."

I went to Mam and passionately questioned her.

She swore to me that she was not pregnant, just fat.

I believed her. I had more reason to believe her than a stranger.

Besides, I wanted to believe her.

But days later, going through her correspondence as usual, I came across a most suspicious letter. It was from Uncle Max -"Motty" - who, having passed his dental exams at long last, was working outside Leeds as a locum.

The letter quite clearly congratulated Mam on her pregnancy and wished her an easy birth. I was disgusted.

Talk about treachery! They were liars, both of them, Mam and Dad. Worse, they had decided that I wasn't good enough for them. They didn't want me. What had I done wrong?

Why wasn't I enough for them?

What did they expect a baby would give them that they hadn't got already?

I could see no sense in it. My world had lost one of its foundations. I must have spent night after night worrying about my failure to satisfy them, their failure to be satisfied with me.

Finally the time came for Mam to go into hospital to have the baby she wasn't going to have, and Mrs Baker from up the street was brought in to look after me and Dad. She tried to pack me off to bed at six, which wasn't my bedtime, objected to my favourite radio shows and nagged nonstop. The food was all wrong, the house was all wrong. Dad looked as glum as I did but it served him right. Mrs Baker was horrible. But Dad could always go off to the pub or the Working Men's Club. I was stuck with this harridan who took my books from me, then complained that I was always picking my nose. What else was there to do?

Mam never had babies easily. She was in labour with Betty for three whole days, causing great concern to the family. The birth exhausted her. When she finally came home, two weeks later, bringing the baby, she seemed to have little time for me. To be honest, she had no time for me at all.

The baby was born sick and it had great staring blue eyes and it was ill. It was always ill. It didn't seem to want to live. There were at least three different things wrong with it. It screamed a lot and when it wasn't screaming, it whimpered. According to my mother, it was crying because it was in pain.

The baby was breast-fed in front of me. "Before your very eyes," as Arthur Askey said. But the baby had no appetite and turned from the nipple, or sicked up all over Mam's shoulder. What went down and what came up were almost equal.

When the nipple slipped from Betty's mouth, an arc of milk leapt across the room. Mam had so much milk and the baby took so little that she was soon engorged. So the doctor ordered her to pump out the milk using a little machine with a big black rubber ball. When she squeezed this, out flowed the milk into a glass bulb attachment.

She then had the nerve to give me the milk and tell me to throw it down the sink. What a waste!

I could hardly believe my ears.

I offered to drink it to save waste. She behaved as if I'd offered to drink her blood. "Throw it in the sink!" she screamed hysterically. This was ridiculous. I'd seen with my own eyes where the milk came from, and if it was good enough for the baby, it was good enough for me.

I was very jealous, and equally curious. So after throwing the stuff away a few times, just to lull her suspicions, I took a long drink of breast milk between the living-room and the kitchen sink. It tasted of *nothing.* One of life's deepest disappointments. It wasn't subtly sweet and creamy like cow's milk, just a grey-flavoured liquid.

Maybe it would have tasted better if I hadn't been bottle-fed. And maybe not.

The baby brought the customary chores of nappy-washing, nappy-changing and nappy-drying. Though we had a small electric boiler installed to give us hot water, it was never enough. Ordinary washings in the morning, hands-face-arms-and-neck, had to be supplemented with a kettleful of hot water. On bath nights, we had to use every pan and kettle in the house to get a lukewarm bath.

This was without benefit of the baby. Of course she made life much worse. Having babies around was discomforting. Your mother was always washing nappies, hanging out wet ones and taking them down again before the rain had a chance to wet them all over again. Then she put on a clean nappy and the baby cried and dirtied it and so on and so on...

Conversation was dominated by the oft-repeated horrors of the baby's birth. Times without number I'd been told of my own arrival, the policeman sent to bring Dad to Mam's deathbed, the fact that having me nearly killed her. To this encouraging saga of childbirth was now added Mam's three days of labour in hospital, her screams of agony - the boredom of it all. The result of all this suffering was the wailing bundle they called Betty. She was the only baby in the maternity ward who had a pointed chin. This was to them, but not to me, a source of pride and distinction. "You'd know her anywhere," the Sister was quoted, "we've never seen such a pointed chin on a baby before."

I was not impressed. If this was supposed to be my little playmate, why wasn't it playing?

However, all these horror stories didn't affect one whit my determination to have twelve children. I must have imagined some alternative form of childbirth - instant baby.

And all the time, the talk of war grew louder.

REGENT STREET

Leeds expanded rapidly in the mid-nineteenth century but since housing was unregulated most of it was built by speculative private builders. The area leading from North Street to Regent Street was laid out by Bischoff in 1809, hence the road names Trafalgar, and Nile Streets; commemorating two of Nelson's victories.

*

As my Mam was struggling to care for the wailing ailing baby, I took more interest in life outside; the Saturday visits to the big house in Harehills became more important. Here lived my mother's family, the Zeretskys. Of Mam's three surviving sisters, only one had married - Auntie Dora. She was a sweet, soft woman with the typical Zeretsky cupid's bow of a mouth. She wed a kindly man "in the tailoring" and they had two girls, May and Rosalind. To me they were beautiful and dearly loved. Their house was a one-up-and-downer, so small that we hardly went there. We met in Harehills Terrace at weekends, the whole family.

Auntie Fanny and Saidie were so complete a twosome that in my innocence I took them to be married. Saidie had vivid good looks but it was easy to see why Fanny was still a spinster. She was very fat and quite plain. In those days if you were fat, that was that. Fanny accepted fatness as her fate and didn't diet until she was about seventy, under doctor's orders.

Both Fanny and Saidie had a certain raw energy. Being factory hands they liked to swear. Their stories were of hostile encounters with bosses and foremen and how they *told them off.* They were large women. In winter they liked to stand in front of the fire, hitch up their skirts and warm their bottoms.

Fanny was definitely the leader, not only by age but by character. She used to say, "Shite, excuse me," very often. It was understood that this was a genteel version of "shit", though to me it always sounded worse. They also used the Yorkshire "bleddy" instead of "bloody". Once as I sat underneath the dining table and counted twenty-nine bleddies in five minutes. These endless sagas of battles on the factory floor involved other women, usually wicked as witches in a fairy tale, and demonic machinery. Because they were on piecework most of their working lives, their conversation went something like this:

"So I says to 'im, I says, you bleddy liar, you never told me what was wrong with the bleddy machine. Well you can bleddy well give it back to 'er, she done it in, she can use it. 'im and 'er both are just pieces of shite. Excuse me. Do you think 'ee could look me in the eye? No 'ee could not. Could 'ee look me in the eye Saidie?"

"No 'ee could not. "

"And you a married man I says to 'im. Don't think we don't know why *she* always gets the best machines I says straight to 'is face din I Saidie?"

I listened fascinated to their conversations and couldn't understand why I wasn't allowed to bleddy my way through life. You could see they enjoyed every minute of it. But my parents never used "shite" and the worst I ever heard Dad say was "bleddy fool" and "silly bugger". The dreaded 'f' word I didn't hear through the whole of my childhood though I saw it chalked up on walls.

Fanny and Saidie gave me sixpence a week pocket money, a large sum in those days but I wasn't allowed to spend it. It was *silver*. All silver was taken to school on Monday morning, to be put into the Yorkshire Penny Bank. What child would need a shilling a week? You could get a lucky bag for one halfpenny with a sherbet dip inside it!

Uncle Gaby too was unmarried, still living at home, and my favourite hero. When the conversation turned to politics, he would stand in front of the fire, the correct place to hold forth, and expound on Stalin and Hitler. "Stalin will stand up to Hitler," he used to say, as the family grew steadily gloomier. The British upper classes were not too keen on standing up to Hitler. Many of them hoped that Russia and Germany would turn on each other and wipe each other out. All Britain had to do was stand aside, wait for the end and then take over Europe. The loss of a few million Jews in the process would be all to the good.

So for the moment, Jews in England were safe. While Stalin was trying in vain to make a pact with Britain against Hitler, hopes were high. Failing the pact he needed, Stalin simply switched sides and signed with Germany instead. The talk at Harehills Terrace was all of conscription and war in Europe - which was the best to join, the army or the navy? Alec in London was going into the Rifle Brigade, his father's regiment.

In Leeds Uncle Gaby became very quiet and stopped defending Stalin. Seeing him sit silent by the fire, his shoulders hunched like an old man's, frightened me. I remember a phrase from this era: Hitler was going through Europe "like a knife going through butter."

When Chamberlain came back from Munich with his "peace in our time" promise, no-one believed him. In June 1939 I was seven years old. People in Leeds were saying, "They're only waiting till the harvest is in, then they'll declare war." So young but I remember that.

What a queer bit of knowledge for a child of seven to acquire! But this was the correct thing. You get in the wheat first, then you declare war. And the weapons talk was all about gas - poison gas. The Germans had used it in the last war, they would use it again. Everyone was sure of that.

Everyone was right, and everyone was wrong. They used it again in the death camps, not on the battlefield. The gas had proved too dangerous in the open. When the wind changed it blew back from the Allied lines onto the German trenches. Besides, with their new motorized divisions and stronger fire-power, the Germans didn't need gas. But we were not to know that.

We were all issued with gas-masks. Mam was too busy nursing baby Betty through her nonstop ailments to be able to collect them, so my headmistress at school, a lovely lady called Miss Strawbridge, took me into town to be fitted with a mask. It was like a cut-short elephant's trunk that covered your face, mostly black rubber. But the part that worked, that filtered out the poison and let you breathe air, was a shiny metallic sieve at the end of the trunk, with tiny white circles cut into it. The gas mask came with a strap attached; the strap went round your shoulder. Summer or winter, rain or shine, it was never to leave my side for years. Without the gas mask, you couldn't go anywhere. This didn't bother me. Like all the other kids, I soon took the gas-mask for granted.

What bothered me was the fact that - everyone knew - it would only work for twenty minutes or so. After that, the filter thing was useless.

I don't know the chemical facts. Maybe it would have worked for longer. But we had to practise wearing them at school where we soon found that twenty minutes in a gas mask, even in ordinary air, was practically impossible.

Your face got scarlet under the rubber, you sweated, you felt you couldn't breathe. It was asphyxiation gassing without poison.

The picture of war in my mind had always been one of grownups hitting each other like children in a large school playground. Now it became weirder still. The scene was confusing: people of all ages and sizes, wearing gas-masks, hitting each other (it was always the same playground) but stopping every twenty minutes to go inside, take off the masks and have a rest. To my mind there *had* to be a truce every twenty minutes - wouldn't everybody be equally uncomfortable? I don't think I understood that war meant killing people. I might have understood that birds and animals die, like the nestlings fallen out of trees that I rescued every spring and faithfully fed with worms, only to have them die after a few days. Yes, I could understand death, but not killing.

*

In June 1939 it was my seventh birthday. You only got one present for your birthday, if you were lucky - and I was lucky. I got roller skates. I'd begged for them because Alan had a pair and they were marvellous. So I was given skates, good ones too. They were adjustable in size and lasted for years. I learned to skate like the wind and with Alan I skated every smooth street for miles around. If my parents had known where we went on our skates they'd have had twenty blue fits. Fortunately, Mam was too busy with Betty-care. Even more fortunately, there was little traffic on the roads in those days. Most fortunate of all, I learned quickly, otherwise my experiments in speed would have ended me.

I soon realised that going downhill gave me speed - this made me faster than any effort of mine could produce on flat ground. The steepest hill nearby, Shepherds Lane it was called, was ideal but for one disadvantage. At the bottom of the hill, just as I'd swoop down at forty miles per hour, was an intersecting road with fairly heavy traffic. Buildings obscured my view on the swoop-down bit, so I could never tell whether a lorry was coming or not.

It is possible to stop a speeding swoop on skates at the bottom of a steep hill. Just. That's one reason I'm alive today.

The people who 'd been wrong about the gas were right about the harvest. War was declared the day before Betty's first birthday.

We were all gathered round the wireless that morning, waiting. My mother cried. Baby Betty cried too, but not because of the war. The rest of us felt nothing but relief.

There's A War On

A few days after the outbreak of war, the family was split up.

Dad joined something called the Rescue Squad. Its full name was Rescue, Demolition and Decontamination Squad; it was an arm of the Civil Defence. He was on duty 24 hours and 24 hours off. He brought home a black book which he studied - and so did we, of course. It had chapters on various poison gases and many more on first aid, splints and such. People were so sure we'd be gassed it was one of the few areas where the authorities were prepared. But Dad's squad was barracked next to the decontamination chambers, in Sheepscar next to the gasworks. A masterstroke - the Germans would only have to knock out the gasworks, a giant building very conspicuous from the air, and they'd simultaneously knock out half the industry of Leeds plus the decontamination squad and its chambers.

We all expected to be bombed. There was some heavy engineering in Leeds, and about half a mile away, on the road to Roundhay Park, the Blackburn Aircraft Factory. But when bombing started after a year of "the phoney war", tons of bombs fell on the East End, Leeds was hardly touched. We weren't to know this. The aircraft factory was camouflaged, painted so its roof was all wavy with greens and browns. Since I could see clearly that it was still a factory, it was hard to believe the Germans wouldn't.

All the street lamps were turned off, many windows were sandbagged to prevent injuries from flying glass. And every pane of glass was crisscrossed with strong brown sticky paper. In every street there was an Air-Raid Warden, usually someone past military age, who went around nightly checking to make sure that no chink of light would get through the curtains when they were drawn. People said that the light from a cigarette could be seen from the sky three miles away. I don't believe that now but I certainly did then.

Convinced Leeds was in danger, the authorities ordered the evacuation of all women with babies and all children. Mam, Betty and I were evacuees. This was how it was done.

In country areas considered safe Civil Defence officers inspected every house in every village to see how many additional people it would hold. They weren't very fussy, they couldn't be. A spare room or bed meant space for another child, and of course many beds were empty because people had rushed to join the forces. The Civil Defence knew they had to split up families, but they had to billet the kids and their mothers wherever they could. Better alive than dead, they said.

Many evacuees were not exactly welcome to start with. They often grew even less welcome after a few days.

I went with my whole school. It was a triumph of people engineering; we were all ticketed with our names and true addresses pinned with safety pins to our coats, thousands of us. How they didn't lose a few kids here and there I'll never know. Leeds City Station was swarming with kids; our mothers came to kiss us goodbye; we were loaded onto trains - we didn't know where we were going, and neither did they. But there wasn't too much weeping and wailing, because there was a war on. Mothers, children and teachers alike were all making a conscious effort to be brave. Mothers were kept firmly on the platform; they waved to us as the train pulled out. In Mam's case she was put on another train with baby Betty, still ill, still screaming lustily.

Mam's experience of evacuation was short, sharp and bitter. I can't remember whether it lasted three days or a whole week. People were willing to take her, but not the baby. Betty screamed day and night, and country cottages had no facilities for coping with ailing babies.

My experience was quite different.

I was delivered to an old crone who lived in a ramshackle one-up and one-down cottage surrounded by fields. "Crone" is the correct word. She was stooped almost double, walked with a stick and she looked like the witches in story books. In addition she had a large long growth which drooped down from her throat, something never seen even in fairytale books. This was a goitre, which my dictionary says is "a morbid enlargement of the thyroid gland, often showing as a large pendulous swelling in the neck." It resulted from iodine deficiency, common in that part of Lincolnshire, and isn't seen these days because it is so easily cured. At any rate, she was very old and very ugly.

However, my story books had prepared me to deal with all sorts of unusual people, and she endeared herself to me immediately by asking the simple question: "What does your mother give you to eat?"

Now I would have sworn I was a truthful child. I certainly didn't intend to tell lies. There was no planning in my artless answer, yet this is what I told her: "I live on bread and jam and custard and cakes."

She looked relieved. Only now do I realise the relief was real - it's easy enough for an old woman, an ailing old woman, to make custard and bread-and-jam sandwiches. And for a fortnight that was precisely the menu: bread and jam, custard and cake. I was satisfied, so was she. Soon I was covered with huge red spots of the kind we called "heat spots", a skin reaction to my peculiar diet. But I did not connect the swelling spots with my chosen fare, and there were green fields all around, and frogs in the garden.

I was entranced. I was sitting quietly in the garden when I saw my first frog, and it was beautiful. It put out its tongue and caught a fly exactly the way the nature books said it did, thus restoring my faith in books. I'd started to distrust them because they were full of birds that seemed to be nonexistent in Leeds. No matter how hard I looked I could never find a greenfinch or yellowhammer or even a robin. In Leeds there were sparrows, pigeons, rooks, swans and ducks. Nothing else. All the stuff about eagles and storks and kingfishers might as well have been fairy tales. As for animals, outside London Zoo there were just dogs and cats and rabbits in cages. That was the whole of Nature's repertoire. The chook man came every week to sell Mam a dead chook - you'd hardly call this contact with bird life. Hence the frogs in Navenby proved that the world of nature books really did exist: if there were frogs there might also be hedgehogs and badgers. I was happy in Navenby.

After a fortnight of frogs and custard Mam arrived to claim me, an avenging angel. She was appalled at my scarlet heat blobs and exploded in fury when she heard what I'd been living on. "Custard!" she screamed. "Why did you believe her? Who feeds a child nothing but custard and cake?"

I was dragged away in disgrace and we all returned to Leeds to be bombed. But nothing happened.

*

Don't think that I was a happy, well-adjusted child. About half the time after Betty's birth I was filled with a raging sense of injustice.

School was much the fairest place to be, though I encountered one raving episode of injustice even there. When I moved up from the Infants to Elementary School, we were ruled by a headmistress called Miss Barclay. All our teachers were Misses in those days; married women weren't allowed to go on teaching. The dread was, they might actually get pregnant and stand in front of a class letting all the kids see they were pregnant. This might unhinge our minds. But as the war went on, authority decreed that a married teacher could go on teaching because victory over the Germans was more vital than prudery.

One day an awful girl, name forgotten, accused me of scratching her and produced a badly bleeding arm to prove it. God knows how it happened - we were all scuffling in the queue to go after playtime and I was holding a pencil; it couldn't have produced such claw marks. I was hauled to Miss Barclay's room and charged with the crime. I denied it. Then she stood me in the corner, left me half an hour, took me out of the corner, charged me again and smacked me very hard on the tender part of my legs behind the knees. I still denied it. This went on all morning and all afternoon till I realised I'd never get home unless I confessed. So I did, got one final smacking and went home crying. Not from the pain - she was nothing compared to Dad in action - from the injustice of it.

Mam wanted to know why I was crying.

"Because the headmistress smacked me."

"Then you must have been doing something wrong." With that, she walloped me, on the grounds that I'd been very naughty and I wouldn't tell her what I'd done. Afterwards I looked at my fingernails, bitten to the core as usual, and wondered why Miss Barclay hadn't thought of checking, why I hadn't thought of showing her my nails, and why Mam preferred to believe a teacher rather than me. Then and there I decided never again would I tell her anything about school that could be twisted against me.

Another injustice was being sent to run errands. Being torn from an exciting chapter in a storybook was bad, but being sent to Taylor's was worse. He was an old man who used to feel up little girls. He'd make us wait to be served: in those days it was quite usual for kids to wait until every adult in the shop had been served. At the age of seven, I had no right to a place in the queue: kids just waited. Old man Taylor's aim was to get girls alone in the shop: then his wife would disappear and he'd put his hand up my skirt and try to get into my knickers.

I hated him. I wriggled and squirmed but never dared to protest outright or tell Mam. Luckily he had to stop when other customers came into the shop, but going there and waiting to be "served" was horrible.

Mam knew I hated going but never had the sense to sit down with me and ask quietly why I hated that one shop so much. Maybe she just didn't want to know.

REGENT STREET 1935

Although far from clean, corner shops were a major social amenity. They usually allowed tick - deferred payments - and sold most things. The shop on the left might be a pop shop - pawn broker's - or possibly one selling second hand goods. This picture was taken by the surveyors immediately prior to slum clearance.

Now I come to think of it, what difference would it have made? He was the only Jewish shopkeeper in the district, she was housebound with a sick baby most of the time, and during the war it was vital to stay on good terms with your grocer. He sold pickled herrings straight from the barrel and good black rye bread, Latvian-style, with a shiny crackly crust. So that was that.

I fought with Mam over going to Taylor's, and sometimes when Dad got home dead-tired from work or the Squad, she'd greet him with tales of how badly-behaved I'd been, and he hit me. All he wanted was peace and quiet and a hot meal, but he got reports of defiance and refusals. So he'd hit me, just to shut her up, but he couldn't hit anyone in cold blood: he had to work himself up to a rage to do it, then he hit too hard. One clout from his cabinet-maker's hands would send me reeling halfway across the living-room. He didn't know when to stop. He must have felt trapped, fed up of nights spent nursing the whingeing baby, days at work, coming home to a complaining wife and a misbehaving child. Anyway, one clout would be followed by more; a little girl is an easy target. He'd aim for the head. Within two minutes Mam would be terrified. "Not her head, Jimmy - not her head!" She was scared I'd get brain damage. She'd scream hysterically for him to stop, and her fear infected me. I'd dive under the table, get dragged out from there and take refuge with my head under the marble mantelpiece. It was very good protection for my head but the snag was it left the rest of me at his mercy. He'd soon enough give up then, or Mam would pull him away.

When I was seven he started to beat me with the dowel sticks he kept in my bedroom cupboard. I called them "dial sticks" because that was what the word sounded like to me; they were used in cabinet-making, I don't know what for. He hit so hard that often the stick broke and he'd have to get another from the cupboard. If he could catch me and make me bend over, the stick came down on my behind. This was a rare event. I'd dive under the bed, get dragged out by one leg as often as not while he hit me on the other. I was all over the place. More than the pain I hated the indignity of it. The people I read about in story books never got clouted across the face, chased from room to room and hauled out from underneath furniture while they screamed blue murder. Because of course I did not, could not, stay still and let myself be hit. It hurt too much.

About forty years later I asked him, "What did I do that was so terrible you had to hit a little girl of seven with dowel sticks?"

He was amazed. He answered stiffly, "All my friends had kids and hit them and they turned out all right. I don't know what went wrong with you lot!"

It was true that every kid I knew got hit, one way or another, and Alan's mother was much worse than my dad. She made her kids bend over a chair and leathered them with a strap. Their screams were heart-rending.

The difference between me and Alan was that I read books, and I'd read enough to know that parents should not behave like mine. My standards weren't learned in Hares Terrace, and the more he hit me, the angrier I got. Occasionally I'd come out with a choice piece of invective: brute, bully, idiot. He'd hit harder, but I could see the words hurt him.

After he hit me, I hated him.

I'd swear to myself that I'd never speak to him again as long as I lived. I meant it and tried desperately to stick to my resolution. But I loved him more than he loved me, or so it seemed. I was always the first to give in - he didn't take any notice of my sulky silences. Later, when I became a dreaded teenager, I could refuse to speak to him for months on end. But in the war I could only ignore him for a day or two, then my need to be noticed became too great. Life wasn't fair.

*

Now during the war sweets were rationed. Besides, we kids went by quantity, not quality - and the Quality Street collection was very special. The toffee wrappers were all silver and gold, or clear cellophane with crimson flowers on. When you held them up to the light they glowed and sparkled. It was like looking at stained glass. There were so few things with vivid colours in those days; they seemed as precious as jewels.

Betty and I were given equal numbers of toffees; she ate hers and threw the wrappers away. I saved all mine and rescued some of hers. My stock of toffee wrappers, seven in all, was my treasure. I kept them in my half of the sideboard cupboard and took them out to play with. Betty, about two at the time, saw them and set up a scream for them. When she screamed, the noise was awesome.

Mam came and forced me to give up my toffee papers. I protested, argued, reasoned, wept. No use. "She's only a baby," said my mother. "They're only toffee papers," she said. "You're a big girl now, you ought to know better. She's

your little sister. You ought to love her." She knew very well I didn't. "Give her those papers."

Until she took them from me I didn't believe she would.

If I'd thought her capable of being so unfair, I'd have fled, taking seven toffee wrappers with me. But she wrested them from me and gave them all to that Betty. My heart was split into bits, or so it felt. There was no trust left in the whole world.

For many years after I used to tell the tale to kids and say, "And now, if someone took everything I possess in this world, I wouldn't feel half so bad about it as I did about those seven toffee papers."

And I thought to myself, why bother to have children?

For I knew very well she hadn't meant to shatter my faith and spoil my trust in her for ever. I knew she only wanted to stop Betty screaming; she had not even meant to be unkind. She saw nothing special in toffee wrappers; I was eight years old, Betty was two. Why make such a fuss about bits of paper?

No parents can win. One way or another, children break your heart.

Today I understand the real reason for my grief. She had switched loyalties, as all mothers must, to protect the youngest. I was no longer closest to her heart. I would never be most loved again. And round the core of my love for her, hate grew snugly.

*

LOWER HEADROW

The bays at the front of the Museum and Art Gallery are very plain and contrast with the rooms inside. You can see why. When it was first built, houses occupied the area which is now the ornamental square outside the Gallery. The Gallery could not be seen from the Lower Headrow but faced onto a narrow, mean street.

Our favourite game was played on the tramways.

The game was based on the well-known fact that most homes had gas meters which always needed change. Some took pennies, all took sixpences and threepenny bits and shillings. All the tram conductors were used to mums and dads sending their kids to the nearest tram stops to get change from the tram conductor. They were laden down by leather satchels full of heavy coinage, and there was an unwritten law that any kid could get on a tram and ride just one stop in any direction, ask for change and get off without buying a ticket.

To play the game properly and honourably, which I did, you first had to "borrow" a ten-shilling note from your mam's purse. Alan and I took turns, and as we always returned the note at the end of a busy afternoon, no-one ever discovered our filching. We preferred to play on Chapeltown Road trams; because this was away from our nearest and most usual route we were less likely to be spotted and denounced by neighbours.

Together we'd get on the first tram riding into town, but again we followed an unwritten law; if you were just asking for change and not buying a ticket, you stayed on the tram steps and didn't go inside.

The conductor would spot us and he'd come to meet us, and we'd chorus: "Please mister, could you give us four half crowns for this ten-shilling note?"

You had to change the note methodically, step by step, until you ended up in Briggate with two hundred forty halfpennies.

Then you crossed the road, believe it or not , and step by step turned your ha'pennies into ten shillings, your shillings into five florins, your florins into four half crowns, and you returned home with the ten-shilling note.

A good time was had by all. Most of the tram-drivers were quite happy to get rid of their heavy change, and even the ones who cottoned on and knew very well that we were just playing with money couldn't do more than curse us. "Bloody kids at it again!"

*

Near us on Harehills Lane, near Potty Park, was a huge old house, nearly a mansion. Before the war its garden had high iron railings to keep people out, and the owner must have specialised in growing roses. As soon as war broke out, all railings around parks and gardens were taken away in the great scrap iron drive. They were melted down and used for guns.

Troops were billeted at first in the old house; it would have held at least fifty. But soon they were moved out, they were needed elsewhere. Since it was no one's job to look after the garden, the roses ran wild. They climbed and clambered all over, sedate city roses transformed to ramblers. No one cared who went in and out of the garden, though the empty house was kept well barricaded and locked.

Adam once decided to lead his gang on a raid and capture me. That was frightening. I ran like hell simply because they were all running after me, and I didn't know what I'd done to turn them into enemies. They caught me.

"Let's torture her!"

Adam agreed.

"But not you lot," he decreed. "I'm going to torture her myself. It'll be worse for her that way. I'm going to take her into the rose garden and torture her there."

They agreed. There was something so sinister in the suggestion that it pleased them all. I was too terrified to protest; I thought my final hour had come. I let Adam drag me into a corner of the rose garden.

Very seriously, very gently, he kissed me.

*

For those of us up North who escaped the serious bombings, wartime was the safest and friendliest period of our whole lives. Though we had the blackout every night, we roamed the streets safely in the dark. Murder, rape, child abduction and lunacy were at an all-time low. Everybody hated the enemy so they used up all the spare hatred available, and ordinary people were particularly nice to each other. The more the Germans threatened to kill us all, the more chummy we became with each other. Children were suddenly precious - even the children of the working class.

Why? You may ask. There were two reasons, both political. To fight the war effectively, a coalition government was formed with Churchill as Prime Minister. This meant that the Labour Party could push its policies. For example, no strikes in the mines meant that the miners did get better pay and rations. It was known that the soldiers' morale depended on the welfare of his family back home, so enormous efforts were made to see that babies and toddlers and children got the best of everything - in that order. Babies first.

Antenatal clinics sprang up everywhere. To ensure that unborn babies weren't affected by food shortages, their mothers were issued with free concentrated orange juice and vitamins. Once the baby was born, huge tins of dried full-cream milk, fortified with vitamins, together with bottles of cod-liver oil and more orange juice, were practically hurled at the mother. When the twins arrived in 1942 the whole family got the benefit and drank National Health orange juice for years.

Once every few weeks tropical fruit such as bananas and oranges arrived, but when a ship did get through - and the Merchant Navy risked their lives every voyage - again it was families with children first. While the upper classes wrung their hands at the deprivations they were suffering, the working class had never had it so good. Nurseries were established for factory hands and the toddlers were

cared for up to ten hours a day, well-fed too. School dinners were served almost everywhere, two courses at a rock-bottom price - subsidised, of course, so that kids of school age were eating better than their parents. School dinners were off the ration.

America sent us food by the shipload under a plan called *Lend-Lease*; this meant we didn't have to pay for it until after the war. Though it was all dried or tinned, the entire population of Britain had cause to be grateful. We had lots of dried potatoes, dried eggs, dried peas, and at school we'd be served tinned peaches and custard for dessert. Housewives learnt scores of new recipes based on dried ingredients. Lord Woolton, the Minister for Food, was always inventing new recipes which tasted nothing like their full-flavoured, undried, untinned prewar counterparts. There was an awful dish called *Woolton Pie* created in his honour.

Each person, during the war and for years after, was allowed only three quarters of a pound of sweets per month. There was a page of *points* in your ration book; I became expert at sneaking this book, bounding at top speed to the nearest sweet shop and returning the book to its place. Mam was always wondering why she had fewer points less than she'd thought.

*

PORTLAND CRESCENT

Leeds Corporation started early with municipal planning and were buying properties for compulsory slum clearance as early as the 1870s. Council surveyors' pictures like this one give insights into conditions before people were moved out and put into council housing.
The houses in this 1934 picture were demolished to make way for a municipal car park.

I thieved frequently from Mam's purse or Dad's pockets, but mind you, I was careful not to push my luck too far. I made sure the purse was full of coins before I extracted my loot. Notes and large silver were quite safe from me. I went on stealing for years and never got found out; I also stole from a vast and wonderful department store in the city centre, called Lewis's. Here I stole only one item, notebooks for stories and cataloguing the universe. And I used only one technique.

I bought one and I stole one, never stealing without buying. In the war, paper bags weren't supplied with small purchases, and I'd simply point to a pile of notebooks, hand over the money to pay for one and walk away with two. My school desk was filled with stolen goods.

At home we were always busy - we sewed and darned and darned again, and while knitting or darning we listened to the wireless, and waited for the fish shop to open. I wish I could write a rhapsody about what fish and chips meant to a wartime child. If I were a musician, I could produce an opera.

Fish wasn't rationed, so theoretically you could eat fish till you burst, but in fact the men on the trawlers were risking their lives, and half of them had gone into the navy. There was only enough fish for the corner shops to open three or four times a week. Not during the day, only at night. Then there might be enough fish for an hour or two but never enough for everyone. At least twice a week, Mam would send me to the fish shop to stand and queue for hours.

I loved the drama of it. When the shops had fish, they'd put a notice in the window: "Frying Tonight." In the blackout, the nights were beautiful, crisp, ice-cool. The moon and stars could be seen as clearly as here in the outback of Australia. Huddling together with others in the queue, pressing against the shop window at least an hour before it was due to open, counting, I'd wait in hope that there'd still be fish left when it got to my turn. As the cold began to bite we shuffled to keep warm.

Then, noises inside; voices. The clatter of pans. And in spite of the blackout, a kind of glow reaching out from the windows of the little shop.

At last, the heavenly smell of fish and chips frying. Yet this was only the end of the first act - they wouldn't let us in until they were ready to serve. When they did I'd listen to every order, tremulous with fear of some spoilsport ahead of me ordering "eight large fish and chips please." All with salt and vinegar. That wasn't fair. The kind of fish was totally unimportant. There were only three kinds of fish in the real world: sardines and salmon, which swam about the sea in tins, and fish that got fried - they were the best.

I went early so usually got served. "Four fish and chips please and salt and vinegar." With the heat of the parcel warming my hands, I'd run home hell-for-leather. "I've got them!" Triumph mingled with the aroma. We ate them with our fingers, gourmet food. I'd swap every restaurant in Paris or Sydney for the Leeds fish and chip shops of my youth.

When the nights drew in we'd gather round the radio. Tommy Handley in *ITMA* had us in fits; there was Funf, the comic German spy, and Mona Lot - "It's being so cheerful as keeps me going." We promptly nicknamed Betty Mona Lot. Monday nights were for detective plays with Inspector Stanley.

QUARRY HILL FROM LADY LANE 1904

Although this picture looks rather romantic this area was designated unhealthy well before Quarry Hill Flats were built on the site. By 1919 Leeds had a Municipal Housing Policy. The council estates were a practical response to Prime Minister Lloyd George's call for a 'land fit for heroes'.

It's Monday night at eight o'clock,
oh can't you hear the chimes?
It's time to sit upon your easy chair,
And settle by the fireside,
take up your Radio Times,
For Monday Night at Eight is on the air!

Whatever "they" chose to broadcast, we loved it all. There were shows such as *Much Binding in the Marsh* that made fun of the armed forces, shows designed to educate the public, such as the *Brains Trust*, game shows so idiotic that even a child could follow them. In *What's My Line?* a team of experts had to guess a contestant's job. "Experts" in this case meant expert at guessing and not much else. It turned out that Britain had umpteen people with bizarre trades: they boiled pigs' ears, sliced bananas sideways, unbolted old tanks and in general took our minds away from the war. One man was even a sagger-maker's bottom knocker. When he revealed his job everybody laughed - in those days the mere mention of bottoms was hilarious.

But in the shelters we didn't rely on outside entertainment, we sang to keep up our spirits. There's nothing like singing for stiffening the morale.

Down in the shelter, first we'd all fall upon the sweets that were kept there to comfort the kids, sucking barley sugar and acid drops, sharing out a bar of chocolate. Then we'd start our repertoire and as a family we could go on for hours. We'd start with the Cockney favourites: *Down at the Old Bull and Bush*, *Two Lovely Black Eyes*, *How much is that Doggie in the Window?*, *My Old Man Said Follow the Van* and a dozen more of that ilk. Then we'd get on to the war songs - *Run, Rabbit, Run*, *Bless 'Em All* and *We're Gonna Hang out the Washing on the Siegfried Line*. Gradually these got more sentimental, with all Vera Lynn's top hits learnt by heart, as we assured each other that *There'll Be Bluebirds Over The White Cliffs Of Dover* and *A Nightingale Sang in Berkeley Square*.

If the all-clear hadn't gone, we'd reach the Irish songs. Some there were that we all sang, like *When Irish Eyes are Smiling* and *The Mountains of Morne*. But there'd come a point when we fell silent and then Mam reigned supreme. She and she alone could sing *Danny Boy* as it was meant to be sung, and we'd all be quiet, rapt in the beauty of her voice, the melody, the words and the finality of death.

She always ended with *My Yiddishe Momma* and we'd trail back into the house with the war forgotten, songs remaining in our head. They still sing to me today.

*

Sometimes Dad was stationed in Leeds and came home every 24 hours. There wasn't much rest for him. Betty had infected tonsils and a prolapsed bowel; because of the tonsils she caught every germ within a five-mile radius. Normally the doctors would have operated to take them out, but Betty was so weak they were afraid she'd die on the operating table.

She went from measles to chickenpox to whooping cough to mumps, interspersing all these ailments with bouts of pneumonia, each worse than the one before. Mam and Dad did not even dare move her into the cold bedroom at night. She would lie on the sofa burning up with fever; the only nourishment she'd take without vomiting was American condensed milk, trickled over black cracked lips that began to bleed. Even I would be obscurely frightened and run errands back and forth with cold wet compresses and more saucerfuls of condensed milk. They didn't dare leave her at night, either. They took it in turns to keep the fire going and slept on the floor or in armchairs, waking each other up to swap places. And of course, as she survived each attack and grew older, she became even more precious to them. Dad would never give her the clouts he gave me, so she never became defiant and angry, as I often was. The bond between them grew. She'd dissolve in tears at an angry word.

I watched in powerless fury. Worse, she had clever little fingers that could do things mine couldn't. At two years old, she could open the back door - so I had to lift her in my arms whenever I wanted it unlocked. Mam and Dad jeered at me, "She's got more brains in her little fingers than you've got in your whole body." Why they were so stupid, I don't know. I hated her already; no need to add fuel to the flame.

*

When the Blitz began in London, the authorities stayed in shock for months. Dad's Rescue Squad was still in Leeds while Coventry and the East End took the

brunt of the battle. Finally the brass hats came to their senses. Dad was moved down to London and his parents and sisters came up to Leeds - all four of them in our two-bedroomed house.

Those were overcrowded days. The big bedroom was given over to the family from London. Sally and Hetty were working and waiting till they were old enough to go into the army. Bobbie and Zaidie were in their fifties - ancient to my eyes - and Zaidie ruled the whole house, including my mother. I never thought to challenge him. Once he took a strap to Sally because she spent some of her own wages on a pair of nylons! Nylons were a wicked American invention, whores got them from American soldiers. Sally wept and screamed after he'd belted her, and lay on the bed kicking her legs in fury.

Their visit didn't last long. The East Enders hated Leeds, were miserable away from Stepney, preferred to risk their lives in the Blitz. Leeds to them was primitive, unreal. The natives spoke a different language.

So they left Leeds and spent the rest of the war in London, though bombed out three times, most nights spent in underground shelters. Sally and Hetty were soon in uniform and moved all over Britain by army orders. They were rewarded with freedom from a patriarchal tyrant.

From this brief time I remember two facts. First, when the sirens went and we all had to crouch in the cupboard beneath the stairs, Sally and Hetty turned green. They'd been through real bombing, we hadn't. Later on, the Civil Defence built surface air-raid shelters. The drawback was, as everyone said, they wouldn't survive a direct hit. But then, what would?

The second thing I remember was, Mam took my rationed egg and gave it to my grandma for breakfast. Eggs were allocated, not exactly rationed: every week or so there'd be an *allocation* depending on how many eggs were available. Children got priority. Grownups were lucky to get one egg per week. So, Mam's stealing my egg to give it to Bobbie was rank treachery.

I got revenge by carrying tales to the only ones I knew who were still on my side: Bobbie and Zaidie. As revenge, it was effective. A furious Bobbie wiped the floor with Mam in Yiddish first, then English. All the way home Mam pushed Betty's pram with one hand and hit me with the other. I didn't care. I got my own eggs in future. I wanted my rights; if she didn't love me as she loved that Betty, at least I would have what was justly mine.

ROUNDHAY PARK OUTDOOR POOLS

When William Nicholson Nicholson died in 1868 the Roundhay Estate went into liquidation and was eventually bought by the Corporation in 1871. Roundhay Park, filled with mazes, grottoes, waterfalls and lakes, had a major tram terminus and was three miles from Briggate. The park proved very popular with Leeds people throughout the early part of this century and had an elaborate guide book which described its walks and amenities.

My uncles had vanished from the big house. They were all in uniform "somewhere in England", and came home on leave with presents and, in Gaby's case, a wife called Valerie. She was Jewish but Welsh. From the moment my aunts discovered that she had hair growing between her breasts, they deemed her both witch and bitch. They shuddered at the sight. For my part, Valerie really was a bitch, but not because of her hairy breasts. She had a lovely, lilting voice that I instantly disbelieved, a voice that matched her face - both too good to be true. In my opinion people who called others "Darling" were up to no good. You called people "Love". Proper married couples behaved like Mam and Dad; they quarrelled with each other. I was a dour little realist.

Once I went across the road on some errand to Auntie Addie and Uncle Victor; he was still at home because he worked in the aircraft factory. I found them kissing each other in the kitchen. Immorality! Why were they kissing when they were married already? Years later - at least ten years later - they got divorced and I was no whit surprised. Kitchen kissers - not to be trusted.

Now my parents did the right thing, quarrelled all the time, thus keeping a stable relationship. I myself made sure I married a man who was good at quarrelling. Once feeling slightly bored I challenged him, "Let's have a quarrel. Nothing serious - just a small one."

"Certainly not," he answered instinctively. "What a crazy idea!"

*

Until now, I didn't know I had a really happy childhood. Now I think, here I am making World War Two sound like an extended picnic with community sing-alongs, but in my childhood, the happy bits somehow got telescoped into the past. There was also thievery and lies. Yet when I search my soul to discover any traces of guilt about stealing money from Mam and Dad I don't find them. I never did feel guilty and I don't now. I've tried to feel guilty and given up. I've tried to find out why I don't feel guilty, arguing with myself. "Perhaps I didn't know what I was doing?"

"Nonsense," says my conscience. "You knew very well, look at all the precautions you took against being caught."

"Well, as no one ever found out they were being robbed, it was a perfect case of victimless crime. So no wonder I don't feel guilty."

"It was very wrong all the same," says Conscience.

"Yes it was, I agree, but wasn't I careful and clever all those years ago? If I'd been greedy about stealing, I'd have been found out."

"You could have ended up in the Juvenile Court," says Conscience sternly. "It's just because there was a war on that no one cared about petty crimes."

Now I do agree with my conscience here. But I still can't make myself feel guilty. Maybe I thought I had the right to everything Mam and Dad possessed; but then I have no illusions, Lewis's wasn't an extension of my family circle.

Life has many small mysteries, and stealing money successfully could have been, but was not, my vocation. Just as the hat-shop led to no interest in hats, the constant pilfering from Mam's purse and Dad's pockets led to no interest in larger hauls. I was careful, but I was lucky too.

I have been lucky all my life.

*

Since Hitler had so foolishly attacked the Russians, Stalin and Communism were now officially Good Things. Rumour had it that the Russkis were coming to help us, with snow on their boots. They didn't arrive, but the Yanks did. If you followed them around - they wore expensive tailored uniforms - and chanted, "Got any gum, chum?" they'd supply you with some.

Though we weren't too keen on chewing gum - this was the era of Liquorice All Sorts, Dolly Mixtures, Jelly Babies and Treacle Toffee - we lost no time testing the report, and found it was true. We came upon a group of Yanks at the tram stop opposite Harehills School and set up a rhythmic, "Got any gum, chum?"

Looking more bored than embarrassed, one of them eventually threw several packets of gum at us; these landed at our feet. We felt we'd participated in some strange foreign rite. No doubt America was full of chanting children who had gum hurled on request. Having verified the rumour, we didn't bother with the Yanks again. The same could not be said of Adam's mother - she made a packet. They were always coming and going to her house, and though my mother steadily became more hysterical if I spent a few minutes over there, I was too innocent - perhaps too dimwitted - to work out why. I thought Mam was behaving like a lunatic. Auntie Millie dressed nicely, had long hair down her slim shoulders and looked at least ten years younger than my dumpy mother.

Furthermore, her house was full of pornographic literature.

At any opportunity I would nip into Adam's for a read; the books in question were stuffed behind cushions in the living room. But I was a quick reader, becoming quicker by the day, and I could read a lot in five minutes. Most of what I read was beyond my understanding, but not all, and it did upset me, and it did corrupt. In the books at Adam's house sex was associated with whips and lashings and incredible violence. I wanted none of it. But I'd go on reading with sick fascination long after I registered my own fear and disgust.

Later I learned to deal with this by simply refusing to open any pornographic book. At the time though, I was a sitting duck. The amount of damage these books did to my sense of "me" I can't begin to measure. They were warnings against men, and combined with Dad's sudden bouts of violence to put me on my guard against the whole lot of them. Luckily Adam and all the other boys in our street didn't fall into the category of "men". They were just normal human beings.

*

Another horror story concerned my mother's library books. She knew that I read everything brought into the house, and when she took out a book which was bound to upset me, she did her utmost to hide it. By the same token, I knew whenever she had a book that I ought not to read, and did my utmost to find it. In this case I wish I hadn't succeeded, but I did. It is almost impossible to outwit a really determined child who is also clever.

This book was AJ Cronin's *Hatter's Castle*, the most powerful novel I'd ever read. In a scene of such vivid violence that it left Millie's pornography at the starting gate, the heroine's father kicks her in the stomach when she pleads with him on her knees. She's unmarried and pregnant - he drives her from home in a snowstorm. Her labour is short and agonising, she takes shelter in a barn, the baby is born dead. And that's for starters.

Added to what I already knew of childbirth, my own and Betty's awkward arrivals and the snatches of gossip heard from neighbours, that book was as good as a course in how to avoid having babies. From then on I could never visualise

SHEEPSCAR LIBRARY

The 1919 Libraries Act allowed councils to use a penny rate to build and stock libraries. Sheepscar Library, Gloria's local library, opened in 1938. As this picture shows, it was a rather soulless place but nevertheless essential in a working class district. Without Sheepscar Library Gloria would have remained at best half educated.

myself in labour without supplying the snowstorm and the barn.

Mam had taken the precaution of hiding this book on the top shelf of the cupboard by the fire. It was high up but I learned to balance chair upon chair. Here too were a couple of booklets from women's magazines, with diagrams on sex, menstruation and childbirth. All baffling. Uterus, vagina, ovaries, Fallopian tubes - all technical stuff. What did it have to do with blood, screams and sobs, dead babies and getting married and/or pregnant? I studied diagrams of male and female sexual organs. The penis was in section. I might as well have stared at a map of the stars.

"When two people love each other very much," said the booklet, "the male introduces his penis into the vagina and the sperm are ejaculated and swim up the vaginal canal." There was the Suez Canal, the Panama Canal and the canals on Mars. And then came the vaginal canal. "When two people love each other very much," what with sperm and ovaries and the lining of the womb, you were liable to end up in a barn in a snowstorm, or in Leeds General Infirmary, which was not a noticeable improvement. You would scream and shriek in agony and then the baby would be born dead - or alive and ill? - or occasionally alive and well. I'm not exaggerating the fear. Central to being born a female in the working class was sexual ignorance.

*

While Dad was away in London or Coventry during the Blitz, my Auntie Renie, Alec's young bride, came up to Leeds. She was pregnant, the baby much wanted and the family hoped that she would give birth safely away from the bombings. Like all the East Enders she hated living in Leeds, so we had little love for each other. She was jealous of me. I was Alec's only niece, and we adored each other, which she resented. After a few weeks she had a miscarriage with all the attendant blood and screams, and the ambulance took her to Leeds Infirmary. When she got back, pregnant no longer, she just lay in bed and cried because the nurses had talked about her "abortion". Not knowing that "abortion" was the technical term for what had happened, Renie thought they were accusing her of trying to kill her own baby. Mind you, so many of the respectable married women of Hares Terrace were expert at inducing their own abortions that the nurses would have been right nine times out of ten. Soon afterwards, Renie went back to London, there to produce amid all the bombing two normal children: my cousins Ronnie James and Estelle.

My bed, however, was not left to me for long. For some reason I can't remember, if I ever knew it, Phyllis came to stay with us. She was a factory hand and swore like a trooper. She didn't stay long but left to marry a lugubrious-looking creature who said very little and was henceforth to be known as Uncle Billy. On family visits the two of them would sit together, both with rather long noses and very receding chins, looking like cartoons. Phyllis did all the talking and all the swearing - enough for three or four - she was notorious in her own right. An exceedingly fast worker, she was the envy of all the other factory hands but the bane of any workshop. Phyllis quarrelled with anyone and everyone at work. It was her especial delight to recount the tale of her battles in detail, always finishing up with, "And I wiped the floor with 'im" - *'im* being the luckless manager or even owner of a small workshop. She got away with murder and she was never out of work.

When Phyllis left, I was not allowed to sleep alone. Sister Betty graduated from her cot to my bed in the little bedroom.

Now Betty was a cold child and - due to her many illnesses - dreadfully thin, a bag of skin and bones with great blue eyes, a peaky witchy appearance and shivering skin. By contrast I was - and am - cuddly and warm. Even today I can feel the warmth of my own blood in my own toes. "Nothing wrong with your circulation," say the specialists with respect. Because Betty went to bed before me, bedtime became even more tense than it was already.

Indescribable dangers lurked for me between the light switch and the bed, so when I turned off the light at the door I'd gasp in peril. This was the only time I feared the dark. Out in the streets I was safe enough, in bed I was secure; at the door by the light switch there was no danger. But between the door and the bed...

I didn't imagine anything in particular, just something there, waiting. If I wasn't quick enough, it would get me. That's why I took three flying leaps straight into bed - to be held by cold, clammy, shivering Betty. She was quite shameless about it. "You're like a hot water bottle," she said. "I'm so cold and you're all lovely and warm."

So I was, but she cooled me down.

A year later, still a bag of bones, Betty was taken to see a Great Man at Leeds Infirmary. He was more than a doctor, he was Mr Viner the Specialist.

In those days it was a real occasion when the working class got to see a specialist, so every detail of this momentous meeting was memorised and recounted by Mam again and again. Mr Viner was teaching a whole class of medical students. Mam waited for hours, but eventually the moment came. Betty was presented for inspection, all skin and bones. Her case notes and medical history were deeply discussed in front of Mam and the patient.

The students agreed that her infected tonsils were a serious problem. Every germ for miles around homed in on them, yet such was her state of weakness that she might not survive an operation. They also agreed that the prolapsed bowel meant she couldn't retain enough nourishment from her food.

But what should be done? Here they argued. Some spoke up in favour of risking the operation, some suggesting courses of medication.

When they had all finished, the Great Man spoke.

"Gentlemen," - for there were no ladies present - "you are all wrong. Look at this child, will you? She will not survive an operation. This child needs building up. Mrs Benjamin, take your daughter away, put her on Agarol," (the mildest laxative in the market, sold at every chemist's) "build her up for a year and bring her back, and then we'll operate."

Thus the Great One.

So Mam took Betty away and Built Her Up...

*

The twins were born the night before my tenth birthday, in the big bedroom.

I went up to see Mam when she was in labour, being walked round the room by two aunties. "Come on, Freda," they urged her. There wasn't much room for walking.

She seemed all right when I talked to her. I forget what she said - something like, "Don't worry, I'll be alright."

I was worried nevertheless. Not about Mam herself; I never thought she could die. She was immortal, like Dad. I was worried because the baby might turn out to be a boy. And I had good reason to worry. I now knew what I hadn't suspected

ENTRANCE VESTIBULE, DEWSBURY ROAD LIBRARY

At the end of his life the Scottish born American Industrialist Andrew Carnegie had provided 2505 libraries throughout the English-speaking world. This is one of them. It contrasts nicely with the architectural severity seen in the Sheepscar building.

before Betty's birth. Boys were the preferred sex. Boys were what they wanted, and boys had to have an education. Girls didn't. Girls were better left uneducated, to work in shops and offices. At best they could marry rich boys who'd been educated at university. If the next baby was a boy, I wouldn't get to high school, let alone university.

My prayers were answered: identical twin girls.

*

Although I prayed I'd already decided there was nothing up there to be prayed to. I'd given up believing in God at the age of six, faced by two opposing frameworks -you couldn't call them teachings, or even religions. Home and school simply contradicted each other.

Religion at home consisted of a number of don'ts and a range of delicious foods; apple strudels, matzo, sponge cake. At the Jewish New Year we were always hauled off to the shull. 'Synagogue' was a crazy word invented by Christians to humiliate us; the 'syn' bit was the giveaway. They probably imagined we went there to sin.

Once at the shull, our mothers talked to each other all through the service. Most didn't understand the language, you see. They couldn't follow the service but went there anyway to show off their new clothes - everybody got new clothes for the New Year - and to see each other's children, and to discuss the price of fish in Leeds Market. It was always too high. There were a few devout ladies who understood Hebrew and they prayed at a breathless gabble throughout the service.

All the women were kept upstairs in the gallery, all the men were downstairs, and because boys were almost always sent to heder, a much greater proportion of men took part in the service. The men had all the glory to themselves; the rabbi, the cantor and all the readers were males. A few men who'd escaped indoctrination clogged up the entrances and chatted to each other about the male equivalent of the price of fish. When Dad went to shull, which was rarely, he joined this group.

These proceedings struck me as most undignified and unholy. Every morning at school we had an Assembly, where we prayed to God the Father and God the Son and we sang hymns. I liked the sense of ceremony and the Lord's prayer, with its

CITY SQUARE

The naked lady on the left was Morn, *the companion statue is her sister,* Even. *The statues by Alfred Drury ARA were a gift of Colonel Harding and came in sets of four. In the beginning an attendant was employed to look after City Square and to see that the vulgar did not light matches by striking them on the rear end of these bronzes. When, in the 1950s, the Council indicated that they did intend to replace them there was a popular public outcry, 'Give us back our ladies!'*

impossible request: "Our Father Richard in Heaven, Harold be thy name."

I loved the hymns, always chosen for the greatest child appeal. There was *All Things Bright and Beautiful* and my favourite, one that had divinity, the world and meteorology neatly tied up:

> *We plough the fields and scatter the good seeds on the land,*
> *But it is fed and watered by God's almighty hand.*

Of all those lusty young singers and prayers, no one enjoyed the school celebration more than myself. I sang and prayed with verve and vigour, because I thoroughly approved of the entire universe. I'd written notebooks about it and what I sang made perfect sense.

The trouble came at Christmas and Easter.

That's when my parents said tartly that Jesus was not the Son of God and that he'd caused a hell of a lot of trouble for Jews. He had not saved the world, as anyone could see, and the carols were a load of claptrap. This did not stop me from singing, with great devotion:

> *Away in a manger, no crib for a bed,*
> *The little Lord Jesus lay down his sweet head.*

But I wasn't allowed to sing carols at home. I didn't mind much. We still had Christmas dinner with a turkey, and presents.

The reason I gave up attempting to believe in either religion was purely selfish. One day Mam decided to visit her old friends in Benson Street. I longed to see Doreen again, but these were the days when ordinary people didn't have phones, so there was no way of knowing she'd be home when we got there.

Mam pushed the pram with Betty in it all the way from Hares Terrace to Benson Street in Sheepscar, and all the way I prayed to God to make Doreen be home when we got there. Doreen's house was empty.

It now occurs to me that my reasoning was weird. What I thought then was: I prayed to God. But God did not answer my prayers. Therefore there is no God. Therefore both religions must be wrong. The notion that God could hear my prayers and not oblige never struck me for a moment.

For once I kept my conclusions to myself. God did not exist, but since they claimed he did, there was no point in arguing. Two religions were still available for my enjoyment. The question that occupied me for some time was, which was best?

Christianity scored many points. It had a better story, lots of lovely hymns and more music. On the other hand, it was frightening and vicious when it got to the part about Jesus crucified. Around Easter for years and years the BBC broadcast Dorothy Sayers' play *The Man Born to be King.* It went on the whole week of Good Friday and had horrifically nasty Jewish voices sneering and calling for Jesus' death. "Crucify Him! Crucify Him!" Then kids would follow me in the park yelling, "Who killed Christ? Who killed Christ? The Jews killed Christ!"

This wasn't fair. I hadn't killed Christ. No one I knew had ever killed anyone. We weren't the kind of people who killed other people. And I couldn't run away because I was pushing Betty's pram.

"Get back to Palestine," they'd yell, though not very often.

Not fair again. I hadn't come from Palestine. No one I knew had ever been there; Latvia, Lithuania, the Ukraine, yes. Not Palestine.

In a muddled way I sensed the play and its story egged on those horrible kids. They were being taught to hate Jews, and Dorothy Sayers was as powerful a writer as AJ Cronin. The story of Baby Jesus was lovely, but the end of it was the Crucifixion, nasty stuff. I concluded that Mam and Dad were right. The attraction of Christianity remained, though, and I always envied people daft enough to believe it lock stock and barrel, hook line and sinker. I also rather fancied myself as a nun, kneeling and lighting candles - I was very keen on candle-lighting.

I used to think I was clever to avoid the trap of falling into either religion. But I fell into the biggest trap of all, the unquestioning acceptance of the base of both. Glory, honour and dominion over the earth. In school we never questioned the rape of the earth, the killing of wild creatures. Lumberjacks chopped down forests in Canada; this was a romantic way of life. We saw rivers choked with logs and never doubted that this was good. Trappers killed for furs because God had created animals for us, hadn't he?

All tigers were man-eaters and should be shot, lions attacked hunters and made nice rugs, whales had to be harpooned by brave Eskimos and seamen in small boats, hens gave eggs and cows gave milk. It was all 'giving' in those days. Now I know we do the taking.

Once I saw a film, *Picnic at Hanging Rock*, which perfectly expresses my own bafflement at the human race. Three schoolgirls taken to Hanging Rock on a picnic

have decided to climb the lone cliff. Halfway up they look down and see their friends below scuttling about like ants.

The three on the rock are already doomed, and we know it.

They stare in puzzlement at the people below and one says:

"I suppose they must serve some useful purpose."

I hope so too...

*

The cinema was our weekly delight, and we flocked to the *Gaiety* and the *Clock* urged on by parents who were as eager to get rid of us as we were to enjoy the bliss of deep comfy seats and the thrills of paradise.

The cinema and radio shared the same status in our eyes. Whatever the films, we loved them. I can't remember seeing a bad film in my childhood. They were all lovely, good, exciting - sometimes too exciting but never predictable and boring as I often find them today. The end was always happy, the intervening scenes kept us pinned to our seats with suspense. Oh the relief when cops caught robbers, Indians bit the dust and wicked witches vanished in flames and smoke.

The ritual started at home. Every Saturday afternoon - no cinema on Sundays, by law! - we begged threepence for the Gaiety or sixpence for the Clock. We queued up for half an hour before the film started, kicking and pushing in the queue. Those who were oldest and most deeply devoted to each other, teenagers of twelve and thirteen who'd been courting couples for years, were the ones who hit and kicked most eagerly. I noticed this early and it confirmed my idea that happy relationships were based on mutual aggression. We called each other names, threatened to tell our fathers and mothers, and once let into the cinema filled up the front rows and gabbled with joy. There were always plenty of empty seats at the back; grownups avoided the Saturday matinees. A very few forlorn mothers with babies on their laps sat like little islands in a sea of children.

The management knew their Saturday afternoon clientele and booked films to suit. Trailers and cartoons first, then a longish documentary. We were willing to sit through anything that moved before our eyes. Then the main feature: music played, the curtains went up, all voices hushed and the film began.

Laurel and Hardy made us laugh ourselves sick. Shirley Temple and Judy Garland

CHAPELTOWN ROAD 1950

This district of Leeds has always been an immigrant area. In the early years of this century it was a Jewish district; with a modern synagogue and very good shops. The 1927 Louis Street Synagogue stood almost opposite. By the 1960s very few Jewish families were living in this area. The focus populations were moving out towards Alwoodley.

sang for us, Tarzan of the Apes and Sabu the Elephant Boy awed and amazed us. Lassie Came Home for us, Disney worked miracles for us. When I saw *Snow White and the Seven Dwarves* I was so scared by the Wicked Witch that I hid beneath the seat whenever she appeared.

Nor was Romance neglected. Two types were in evidence: Dorothy Lamour in a sarong drooped over pools of water in sundry islands, waiting for shipwrecked sailors, as a chorus of natives sang *Aloha* in the background. If Dorothy and the hero came together by the pool at sunset, their moans of ecstasy would be punctuated by kissing, sucking noises from the audience. The second form of Romance occurred in musicals. It was understood that a Mountie or prince could well go soft in the head and start yodelling *When I'm calling you-ooo-ooo-oooo* instead of getting on with killing baddies or Indians. This held up the action but the scenery was good.

*

Teenagers were called adolescents, and they had acne and puppy-fat. They suffered from shyness. When they wrote to the magazines with their problems they were told to eat more fruit, wash the face often and practise being good listeners. It was a world shaped by *Woman* and *Woman's Own*, not Jeannette McDonald and Nelson Eddy.

As far as I knew, every house in England got both these magazines every week and they were read more eagerly than the Bible by millions of readers. The moment they arrived, we opened them at the back page - the Letters page - where "Desperate Brown Eyes" or "Unhappy Wife" had written to Evelyn Home. Her sympathetic eyes peered at us from the top corner of the page. Today it's hard to write about those letters without mockery.

The question, "My boyfriend and I have been together for three years and he says he will marry me if only I prove my love for him. I too have physical desires and I long for us to be truly together. Should I surrender to his pleas?"

"Certainly not," the answer, "for if he truly loves you he will wait until you are married. And if he is not willing to wait, better not to wed such a one! For you will certainly regret it."

"Dear Evelyn Home, my fiance pleaded with me to prove my love for him and as we had been engaged for years and he threatened to leave me because I did not love him, I surrendered. Now he says he wants nothing more to do with me, can't stand the sight of me, loves my best friend, loves my sister. But I still love him and want to marry him. How can I convince him to return to me?"

"Leave him, and thank your lucky stars that you found out in time that he was false. You are well rid of him. Look for another, time will heal your wounds, you are still young and not all men are jackals. Cheer up."

"Dear Evelyn Home, my fiance pleaded with me to prove my love and I surrendered. Now he says he can no longer respect me and he is engaged to my best friend/sister/cousin, and I am pregnant! What shall I do? My parents will kill me if they find out."

"Tell them, talk to them. Go to your minister or a trusted family friend, but your parents must know. Try the *f*, get the baby adopted."

The one thing she'd never recommend was divorce. If hubby bashed the kids and drank and had a prison record, you were encouraged to seek a separation in a letter starting, "My dear, it would be wiser..."

With lesser evils than these you were urged to remember your marriage vows, grit your teeth and soldier on. "Pray to God for the strength to forgive your husband. You married him for better or worse, didn't you?"

My favourite letters were complaints from girls who lacked boyfriends. These unloved maidens fell into two categories:

A: "I am vivacious and attractive, the centre of male attention at parties, yet no boy wants to take me out a second time. What is the matter with me?"

"You talk too much," said Evelyn, "you are selfish and conceited. Take up a hobby and learn to be a good listener." Translated, this meant play dumb and act stupid.

But best of all was category B: "Dear Evelyn, I am a very boring person because I never go anywhere or do anything much and my looks are average. I have no ambitions but I want to get married and have children. How can I get myself a boyfriend?"

After years of reading such letters it must have been plain to Evelyn that large numbers of girls wanted to dispense with the frills and get on with the job that nature intended them for; that is, reproduction. They were simply human amoebas who reckoned they'd reached the splitting stage, but they'd landed in a society that demanded more, a mating process that involved another, more selective amoeba. Evelyn was always stern with these hapless squodgies, insisting they should join youth clubs and take up night school and develop an interest in something, failing to recognise that they already had an interest and that's why they wrote in.

Let's be fair, in one area she was helpful. If you sent a self-addressed envelope and sixpence in stamps you could get little booklets with diagrams explaining the mysteries of sex, adolescence and "the change". As there was no hormone replacement therapy in those days women were always writing to Evelyn about their hot flushes and dwindling sex lives. "I feel that though I still love my husband it is hard for me to express my love in physical ways," they would delicately dither.

I read all these letters from early childhood, so they must have had some impact on my psyche. We all read them, girls of every age from six to ninety, though they were the same every week. They never ceased to enthral.

Perhaps, like the ritual games that ended the way they started, the Letter Page was a confirmation that life did not change, that the world did not spin round wildly but stood stolidly on respectable lisle-clad low-heeled legs. I know that when my own marriage was in trouble I had an Evelyn Home in my head insisting that marriage was for better or for worse, that nobody had forced me into it and divorce was out of the question. We did not know then - I learned quite recently - that apparently there were five Evelyn Homes.

*

In the cupboard by the fireplace beneath the alcove, for as long as I can remember, were the books. Ten huge volumes of *Chamber's Encyclopaedia* and eight volumes of a different kind - a *Teach Yourself Everything* arranged in eight progressive stages. It was a selection of courses in Algebra, Art, Chemistry, Spanish, Geography, German and more.

Being such a quick reader I'd often finish my library books and magazines and have nothing to read. So I would reach for an encyclopaedia quite uncritically and go through it uncritically - except that I skipped the German, for obvious reasons. I learned nothing by scanning through Algebra and Geometry but taught myself almost all the Art and English Literature, most of the History and Geography and

NEW VILNA SYNAGOGUE

Leeds' first synagogue was opened in 1846. The Russian pogroms from 1881 onwards sent more and more Jewish refugees into the United Kingdom and by 1900 Leeds had 12 synagogues.
The New Vilna Synagogue, Chapeltown Road, was opened much later, in 1959. It started life as the Kingsway Cinema in 1937 and because of its history is popularly known as the Cinemagogue.

some of the Spanish. I didn't do it deliberately. My only aim was to save myself from boredom, and I absorbed what I read because I couldn't help it.

I took the books in the fireside cupboard for granted and as far as I knew, every kid at school had the same access to information. This wasn't true. Those books were a part of being Jewish.

In 1988 I followed a lady to the top deck of a municipal bus because I liked the look of her dog, and we got chatting. She was the daughter of the salesman who kept the Jewish community supplied with encyclopaedias sold on the never-never. So Dad must have bought them hoping they'd have a boy. They can't have bought them for me because by the time I was nine, my cleverness had ceased to be funny or praiseworthy. Their minds had veered away from education and my parroting: "I'm going to Oxford University" had turned sour. I know this because when the time came for me to "go for my scholarship", they said I was not to sit the exams.

*

In 1941 Leeds City Council decreed something called a "Special Place Examination" for bright children. If you were "picked" they paid for you to go to High School. If your Dad was poor, they paid for all your uniform, and after that they paid eleven pounds per term, an enormous sum, just to keep you in High School. Although I was really a year too young for the exam, my teachers thought I could pass it, and said so. My parents refused to sign the consent form. I cried and pleaded and called them names. My teacher from school, Miss Wilson was her name, walked home with me and talked to Mum. I also have it on good authority that Zaidie in London intervened and ordered Dad to let me sit.

Now in the years that followed everyone blamed everyone else for the fact that I was allowed to win my scholarship. You'd think I was going to high school to take up rape and pillage as a career. Later, when I did well, they all reversed positions. Mam used to claim that she had fought with Dad to let me sit the exam. This was not true. She was pregnant at the time, still nursing Betty through her illnesses and hoping that the baby would be a boy.

On the appointed day I, only nine years old, had to go with the members of the next class up to Allerton High School. Here luck played a weird part in changing my life. The line that divided Allerton entrants from those that went to Roundhay High was just yards away on Adam's side of the street. Allerton High was resplendent, brand spanking new. Completed just before war broke out, for many years it remained the most modern school in the British Isles. It had acres of playing fields, games pavilions, science labs. It lacked nothing - nothing, that is, except a knowledge of how to deal with working class girls.

Allerton had started as a private grammar school. Money for the new buildings came from Leeds City Council, who'd made an agreement that in exchange for the subsidy, one-third of its places were reserved for scholarship students.

I can't describe how beautiful Allerton was in those days. It was all golden oak inside, floors and desks shining new. It was polished, spacious, full of light. And it was surrounded by green, green fields.

In due course a letter arrived announcing the award of a "Special Place" at Allerton. With it went a one-off grant of thirty-two pounds to enable Mam to buy me the school uniform. And oh Lord, that was some uniform!

You had to have one and there was no doing it on the cheap, because green was such an awkward colour to match. Since she was heavily pregnant, Mam's strategy was to march me into that shop and buy every item on the list at least three sizes too big. Money had to last, I was a growing girl, and she assured me she would take up all the hems and alter all the waists and sleeves. But the twins were born in June and I started high school that September. She never got around to it.

*

The twins were not suspected until the day before their birth, June 3rd 1942. It was the day before my tenth birthday and the last proper birthday I had as a child. After that there were three of us to be feted on the same day.

When the midwife announced on June 2nd that she could hear two distinct heart beats and possibly a third, I was so excited I told everyone in my class. When Miss Wilson demanded to know the news, I told her too, "My Mam's going to have twins at least!"

She thought I was lying and made me stay in after school. It was half past four when I got home and Greta was born; by five o'clock Brenda emerged, and at half

past five I was allowed upstairs to see them.

Mam has a lovely memory that I looked into their eyes and said, "Only think, in ten years' time when I'm twenty they'll only be ten years old."

What I actually said was, "Huh. Two more to scream like Betty."

And what she actually replied was, "Get that child out of here before, ill as I am, I get up from this bed and wring her neck."

At half past six Dad came home and the neighbours kindly broke the news to him as he walked down the street. When he was sent up into the bedroom to gaze upon twin scarlet faces, he was bereft of speech. Two more daughters. According to Mam all he could say was, "Tut...tut."

Brenda and Greta they were on their birth certificates, not that those names were used. They were so identical that for years you couldn't tell one from the other without stopping them in their wild capering and examining their ears.

In the womb Brenda's big toe had nestled snugly in Greta's left ear. This had left a toe-shaped indentation in Greta's ear-lobe, the only clue to which was which. Mam could always tell - to her it was obvious - but I gave up and called them both Twinnie.

My reaction to the twins' arrival was different to Betty's birth. They had saved my skin by being girls. If they'd been boys, no matter how stupid they were, my parents would have worked themselves to the bone to see them through university. I'd have been taken out of school at fourteen to contribute to the family income. No doubt about it. The twins had obliged me by being female, and I felt guilty because that's what I wanted. And Mam felt guilty because she'd wanted a boy and even worse, because with two girl babies instead of one, she did not dare get pregnant again. She still wanted to try for a boy, but one man's wages were now keeping six people. She'd have to be content with four girls.

There was one unexpected consolation. The babies were born beautiful. It was soon clear that they'd combined the best features of both families. Also, unlike Betty, they were healthy and thriving. A double pram was hastily bought and stationed in the living room. It was one of my jobs to take them out in this pram. In those days twins were quite unusual, really pretty babies were very unusual, and Leeds people believed that if you put silver under a baby's pillow it would bring you good luck. It certainly brought me good luck!

Wherever I went, admiring women pressed silver sixpences and threepenny bits

POTTERNEWTON LANE

Municipal parks were a major feature of the nineteenth century. Their upkeep was a matter of municipal pride. Gloria's local park, Potter Newton Park, was a comparatively recent development, being opened to the public on 12 September 1901.

on the twins. I helped myself to some of this silver shower - perfect strangers would stop me, peer into the double-hooded pram, remark on how beautiful the babies were, and donate coins. The twins were as good as having a bottomless moneybox.

As the months went by, they grew and loved me; I bottle-fed Greta while Mam breast-fed Brenda, and changed their nappies and sang them to sleep. They adored me. Why shouldn't they? So I loved them in return, because that's how women are with babies. Their need creates a kind of love even if you don't start out by loving, so they love you because you satisfy their needs, and on this ground love grows from day to day.

I was better than Mam at singing them to sleep; I'd take both of them onto my lap and rock them with the popular songs of the day - *Yours till the stars lose their glory, yours till the birds fail to sing* - I mixed in the lullabies of Brahms and Schubert we were taught at school.

"The truth is," Mam would say, "they go on screaming till they're exhausted, then Gloria opens her mouth to sing, they close their eyes in disgust and they haven't the strength to open them." Whatever the reason, they'd sleep for me and not for her.

Now while all this loving was going on poor Betty was suffering torments of jealousy. I hardly noticed. It didn't occur to me that all my past agonies at dethronement were now hers, until an enormous row blew up: she was caught taking a ten-shilling note from Mam's handbag.

I was surprised and impressed. I remember thinking that she was too young to have the sense to steal something smaller. My psychology books said that children who stole were stealing love, and so I informed Mam, who raved and ranted at Betty. Betty flooded her face with tears, both of them were totally hysterical. But fancy daring to steal a ten shilling note!

Next, Betty made an energetic effort to throttle the twins. Literally. I can't remember trying this with her, so it showed originality as well as desperation. We found out because Mam noticed that if Betty was left alone with the twins, even when they were sleeping soundly, a few minutes later they'd be screaming blue murder with red marks round their necks. Mam kept a close eye on Betty. She found her favourite daughter in front of a mirror testing the throttling power of her fingers on her own neck. "Is that what you do to the twins?" Mam asked, and

Betty answered, "Yes."

I've forgotten what Mam did, but the throttlings stopped. They didn't shock me or make me despise Betty. On the contrary, I admired her determination!

After the tonsil operation on which so much hope depended, she was brought home from hospital and lay weakly on the bed upstairs. Soon she called feebly for a glass of water. Mam was too tired to drag herself upstairs.

"Go and get it for her," she ordered me.

"Go yourself! I won't go anywhere for that Betty," I replied.

I expected a fight. Instead Mam gave me a most peculiar look and said: "You're a fool."

The look was not lost on me. "Why?"

"That child adores you. She'd do anything for you. Go on, talk to her, you'll see it's true. And you're too mean to get her a glass of water."

This pleased me but I was by no means believing. It had to be put to the test. So I went upstairs, got the water and deliberately chatted to her. I drew her out about the operation and the hospital, and like a detective observed not just the facts but the way she answered me. She was so eager to please, I knew Mam was right. So: I was loved, adored, worshipped by Betty.

Certain ideas rearranged themselves in my head.

I was no longer Mrs Benjamin's little girl. I was Mrs Benjamin's big girl, and "my sisters adore me," I wrote in my school compositions. "I spoil them and they spoil me." - "You certainly are spoilt," commented one teacher.

She was right.

My attitude to Betty didn't change overnight but knowing she loved me was like money in the bank. I relished the thought, enjoyed the idea of the possible cruelties I could inflict. Just by ignoring her I could make her suffer the way Dad made me suffer, and often as the twins grew up I would tell them stories and preface the telling with, "Betty's not allowed to listen to this."

Betty begged and pleaded to listen. Sometimes I'd be magnanimous, "All right, but remember it's not meant for you, it's for the twinnies." And I would deliberately weave their names into the story and leave out hers.

Allerton On The Hill

If Mam had stayed awake nights for months plotting to ruin my school life, she couldn't have made a better job of it. Originally I took her good intentions for granted, but now I wonder. Did she really not notice that when she sent me off for my first day at high school, I looked like something out of the comics? I was wearing a gymslip that came down to my ankles, a green raincoat that swished against my shoes, and the school hat. Very expensive, it was made of the greenest, glossiest velour you can imagine, with elastic to keep it on in the wildest wind. In my case the elastic was superfluous because the hat came right down over my eyes and I had to keep pushing it up to see where I was going.

She was no angel, my Mam. We sentimentalise and forget the truth.

I had to walk a mile across town to get to the school bus, since Allerton, unlike Roundhay High, was nowhere near a tramline. It was three miles out in the country among fields and exclusive housing estates - villas with rockeries - far from the terraced jumble of streets we knew. Being laughed at by people at the bus-stop was one thing; being laughed at and stared at by a whole bus full of girls was another. Going home, I had to queue for the school buses like everyone else, only there were seven hundred and fifty girls at Allerton and they'd all be waiting at the school gates in orderly lines - which doubled up in giggles when they saw me, Mrs Benjamin's little girl.

I'd never been so miserable before.

I'd never been mocked and teased silly before. I was in a trap.

I had only to complain about school at home, and I'd be taken away from Allerton with the speed of greased lightning. Any excuse would do. They didn't want me at high school. They couldn't have made it plainer. They wanted me to grow up, leave school, get a job, get married.

They wanted me to wash up, clean the floors, change the twins' nappies, take them for walks, run errands. They needed a household drudge, not a scholar, and they didn't pretend anything else.

But it was too late to change me. I was ten, I'd spent too many years with books, desk, library. Everything they wanted me to do meant nothing to me. All I cared about was reading and writing and learning about the universe. I could be forced to wash up, change nappies, make feeding bottles and wheel out the twins in their big double pram, but the damage was done. The life they lived, that they expected *me* to live, was a bore. You had to have children who had to have children so they could have children - so what? They had a cynic on their hands. I wanted to escape.

*

Allerton had a school song:

> *Wind on the upland, field and farrow,*
> *Larks in the sudden silence trill,*
> *White gulls wheel over field and farrow,*
> *Allerton on the Hill.*

Here I had my first Domestic Science lesson. "Hands up all those who have an electric stove in the kitchen at home." Half the class put their hands up. "And hands up all those who have a gas stove at home?" The other half of the class obliged.

That left me.

She was going to pass on, but I put up my hand, eager for information.

"Please Miss, what's it called if there's a coal fire with an oven next to it?"

"That," she said with distaste, "is a kitchen range."

So I was the poor girl who didn't have a proper stove at home, whose clothes didn't fit, who didn't even realise that "Prep Book" was not the book you did your homework in but the book where you wrote down what you had to do. I did so many things wrong that I can't remember them all, but I did one thing right. I would not allow them to tease me. I sank my teeth into their stupid hands. I bit.

The girls teasing me were much older than I was. They had no business to make a mock of me and they certainly hadn't expected to get bitten. I was supposed to put up with it, and put up with it, ad infinitum. They were very refined girls and nobody had ever bitten them before. Fee-paying pupils, see? And here was this slum kid, biting.

They rushed to report me to the mistress on duty. Her name was Mrs Barclay, she taught Biology, and I was lucky. She was one of those married teachers allowed back into the schools as part of the war effort and she'd had more contact with real life than most teachers. Before sending me to the Headmistress to be suspended or expelled or whatever - for no girl had ever bitten another in the

CITY SQUARE 1936

The Queens Hotel is in the process of being built. The original configuration of statues and public lavatories is in place, the War Memorial is still in the square and beyond the railway can be seen two Italianate chimney towers of Hardings Mill.

history of Allerton - she wanted to know why.

I told her. I expounded my philosophy, such as it was. I didn't talk about Hitler and the Mile End Road and the barricades, but I explained that they were teasing me, had been at me for days, and I was not going to put up with it any longer. It was true I had bitten them and I had every intention of biting them again. I would bite them whenever they teased me. Whatever punishment I got, I did not care, it would not stop me from biting them.

She listened to me. Then she called the older girls back and spoke to them at length, separately, for some time. She then sent them away. They did not look pleased with themselves and they never bothered me again.

Nobody ever teased me again.

I think the word went round that I was like Lord Byron - "mad, bad, and dangerous to know." I didn't care, or at least I pretended not to care. My first year at Allerton was awful. I was in Upper 3C and I had no friends.

*

At home, I was kept busy with the twins; no time now for playing in the street with our gang. Alan was still at Cowper Street Elementary. We drifted further apart week by week.

To escape from the whole horrible mess, I took to getting off the school bus at Sheepscar Library, reading rapidly for twenty minutes and taking the tram home. Between the tram-stop and our house I'd take off the green velour hat and jump on it. Mam believed anything I told her about school, so far was it from her knowledge. I complained that the school buses were always late and she soon got used to my turning up at five or half-past. From this I learned that committing a crime would hardly be noticed if it was done every day at the same time.

Next, I learned to read like lightning, get the guts from a book in an hour at most. This still left problems, for twenty minutes isn't an hour - too often I'd find the book I was reading went astray, taken out by a legitimate library borrower. So I learned to hide the current book, and was so successful no one found out.

The problem of homework was almost insurmountable. I muddled along, never tackling the real question: How do I survive in this school when I can't do my homework?

The first week at Allerton I actually tried to do it, and discovered it was impossible. Only one room was warm and well-lit, but it was the living-room and we lived there; me and Mam and Betty and the twins. That's where the radio was on, the babies were crying, everybody was talking. Nobody had any notion that I needed peace and quiet - to be honest, I didn't know myself. I'd never had to do homework before. It seemed simple enough. I had to wait until "tea" was over, because there was just the one table; then I sat down at the table with my books, a pen and a bottle of ink.

One of the twins was crying. I held her on my lap with the arm I wasn't using for writing, but she reached out and knocked over the ink. I tried to concentrate in the bedroom, which was cold. I failed. In the end I realised that school was the only place where I could work in peace

I could get to school half an hour early two or three times a week. I had that precious half hour. The teachers were giving us about two hours' homework to do every night, which meant I had ninety minutes at the most to do ten hours' homework. I was no genius at maths but I knew I had to copy from the others just to get by. Curiously enough, copying was easy.

For a day or two before the subject teacher collected the allotted work, a pile of exercise books sat waiting in the classroom. I would arrive early and copy my homework from everybody else, one sentence at a time.

I do mean, everybody else. The same caution which had kept me pilfering successfully for years made me reason thus: I should not copy from a really clever girl, she would be furious and I'd be found out. Too obvious. I should not copy from a stupid girl; I had to get an average mark that nobody would notice. All my copied work brought me no A's and B's but exactly what I aimed at: C, C- or C+. My copying was noted and resented but caution paid off - nobody bothered to dob me in.

The kind of homework that couldn't be tackled sentence by sentence could be done in other people's lessons. Again, not too difficult because by now I was such a speed-reader that I read the chapter we were supposed to be reading in class long before the others; it was however important not to be found out. I soon worked out that sitting on the back row was unwise, quite apart from the fact that I couldn't see the blackboard from there, having "lost" my glasses. The back row was for talkers and troublemakers. No, it was best to sit near the front but close to

the side, because teachers automatically thought that kids who chose to sit near the front were goodies.

If they saw me writing earnestly in an exercise book, wasn't I just taking notes of the chapter I was supposed to be reading? So I did Geography homework in History, History homework in English, and English at break or the dinner hour. I could have used every dinner hour for homework, but the school library was open every day in the dinner hour!

And what a library. It had drawers stuffed with back copies of *Punch*, every William book ever written, all the Dimsie books and the Chalet School series and, wonder of wonders, the *Oxford Book of English Verse*. When I found that book I was drunk for a week.

> *Oh Western wind when wilt thou blow,*
> *that the small rain down shall rain?*
> *Christ, that my love were in my arms, and I in my bed*
> *again.*

I read *Ode to the West Wind* and *Beau Geste* and *Captains Courageous* and *The Yellow Poppy*. I devoured all the school stories, all the historical romances, all of Shakespeare - up to and including *Titus Andronicus*. I was first into the library every day and last out of it. You were not allowed to speak in the library. Who needed conversation?

Some homework was totally beyond me. Biology, for example, with its complicated diagrams, demanded a skill in drawing that eluded me. Chemistry too was all diagrams, Geometry an invitation to the loony bin. Spatially I am inept. I couldn't copy the homework because I could hardly draw two straight lines together. So I'd wait till I was due for three detentions on the same day, then take the day off.

*

At first I'd spend the entire day at Sheepscar Library, but the staff started to ask questions. Why was I there in my school uniform but not at school? Because I was in quarantine after measles, I explained. But though they swallowed this once, it was clear I'd have to make a move.

GRANARY WHARF

Like City Square, the Italianate Towers - actually chimneys - in the background were the inspiration of Colonel T Walter Harding. They were built in the late nineteenth century. The more ornate one was modelled on Giotto's Tower in Florence and is part of a dust extraction system. The other is modelled on Lambeti's Tower in Verona. Originally this had a more elaborate canopy.

I needed a nice warm place, a library full of books, where I could read all day long in safety. And guess what? The City of Leeds councillors, may their names be praised eternally, provided such a place. It was bang in the town centre above the Central Police Station - Leeds City Reference Library.

Criminal is what I was, criminal is how I felt, but like other criminals I learned to live with the police force. I went in and out of the library, they went in and out of the station. There I was festooned in green velour uniform - never shortened, I just grew into it - a schoolgirl who should have been at school. We co-existed. They were looking for regular criminals, not learners.

The library was huge, it had long oaken tables with reading lamps every couple of feet, lamps that had to be lit even in daylight. There was no taking books from the shelves - you had to go into a special room and look through the catalogue. Every card for each of the thousands of books was written out in copperplate handwriting, some cards faded because they'd been there for decades. You filled in a separate form with your name and address for each book then took the form to the main desk where the assistants hardly bothered to look at you. It was the form they were interested in, because each book had to be searched for in the long galleries around the main reading room. Sometimes they took half an hour just finding the books. For some they had to fetch a ladder and go climbing like goats.

I would stagger to the table with a pile of six or seven tomes, enough to last me the day, and if anyone noticed me at all it would be some bona-fide student giving me a poisonous glance of warning. It meant, "If this dratted kid is going to make a noise, there will be trouble with a capital T." They could have saved their unspoken threats, for I was unspoken too.

Of course I read books I had no business to read. Whoever took my form and issued me with *Psychopathia Sexualis* by Kraft-Ebbing must have been a complete idiot. *Secrets of the Confessional* was another one. The worst bits in both these books were in Latin, because no unseasoned, ignorant mind should be exposed to the horrible carryings-on of grownups. Ha! I was studying Latin at school and though three-quarters of what I read defeated me, with the help of a dictionary I managed to figure out more than I needed to know. Kraft-Ebbing had documented every sexual perversion known to man.

Out of the hundreds of cases that I read, one man remains vivid in my memory. His particular perversion was written in English, because it was less nasty than the others. He got his orgasms by having a fried egg placed very gently on the middle of his stomach by a young girl.

Through the years the memory of this man has comforted me. Whenever I read about another crazed rapist, sadist, fetishist or what-have-you, I recall him. Unless and until the price of eggs rose beyond his reach, he had it made. A fried egg on the belly button may be weird but it's a damn sight more comfortable than some of the horrors I read about.

After taking the day off from school, a note was required to explain my absence. Here artistry and restraint were called for.

Though I could put some teachers off by "forgetting" the note or "losing" it, sooner or later a note would have to be produced. I had more guile than my teachers and often took absence *B* while they were still chasing a note to cover absence *A*. I was, as I realise only now, a dour little realist. Since I could not convincingly fake an entire letter, I would write the sort of thing my Mam had once produced for me, in my own round hand.

> *Dear Miss Blenkinsop,*
> *I am sorry I could not let Gloria come to school yesterday -*
> (the note was always undated) - *as I needed her to help at*
> *home with the twins and her sister. I am sorry but it could*
> *not be helped.*

The signature was faked so well that Mam once found one of my undated undelivered notes and stared at it frowning, trying to remember when she'd written it. "It's from ages ago," I said impatiently.

"But I can't remember writing that one."

Two things I was careful about, for teachers occasionally questioned me about those notes. "Why didn't she write it all herself, Gloria?"

"She never has time, she hates writing notes, she just says to me 'You write it and I'll sign it.' " This was what happened on the rare occasions I was kept away from school legally. The teachers knew from my compositions what it meant to have baby twin sisters and another who was always ill, and Mam stayed well away from school, no Open Days or Parents' Days for her.

I took only one day off at a time. Other girls played hookey for longer but they chose sudden abdominal illnesses, "tummy upsets". I looked far too healthy to go through life having tummy upsets.

I got to Oxford because of the days spent in the Reference Library, for Kraft-Ebbing was not my only fare. There I had myself an entire education. Allerton would have got me easily into Leeds or London University; Oxford required something special. However, I lived years of fear of being found out and expelled for truanting. It was a literal nightmare, my only nightmare. Once I woke up in the morning so certain I'd been expelled I was afraid to go downstairs for breakfast. Only the usual sounds of the twins fighting and Mam shouting convinced me all was business as usual.

I can't begin to calculate the price of living with lies for years on end. And I think today, what a fuss about nothing. While you were complaining at being lumbered with the twins, other kids were being starved to death, gassed to death, bombed to bits. Even without a war going on, I've seen little girls of four in Israel, Arab and Jew alike, lumbered with babies who clutched their skirts at every step, just as the twins clutched mine.

But that was the way it was, for me. I wanted an education, I got twin sisters. Mam used to say, "What you want and what you need and what you get are three completely different things." And here she told us the truth.

I had financial problems too, though these were self-imposed. Poor scholarship girls were allowed subsidised meals for fourpence a day, so every Monday I was sent to school with my dinner money. But every day I was also given a bagel which Mam supplied for my "break".

It didn't take long for me to work out that for one penny a day I could join the "cold lunch" girls who sat at a special table; I ate my bagel and pretended it was all I had for lunch. This brought me 75% clear profit, money left over.

Was I hungry? Of course not. The government had arranged for every child in school to be given one third of a pint of milk per day, free.

Of the seven hundred and fifty girls at Allerton, at least fifty loathed milk and there was no efficient way of forcing them to drink it. On the other hand girls like me were ready and willing to drink two or three bottles. I had to grow quickly because of my uniform so I drank all the milk I could manage. From being a fairly skinny child I bulged out in all directions. Talk about a growth spurt. Within a year and a half I was fat.

EVEN, BLACK PRINCE, MORN-CITY SQUARE

No one is sure why Colonel Harding chose to place the Black Prince at the centre of City Square. It is said that he is pointing to the naked lasses and ordering them to go down Boar Lane and start up the cheap clothing industry.

What did I want the money for? I took money to pay for the replacement of my glasses. I'd smashed the previous lot and authority was demanding that I replace them. It was at this time that I first realised we were truly poor, not just pretend poor. The twin's arrival had plunged us into poverty. I didn't mind being poor. The things I wanted money for weren't for myself. I only wore my glasses when forced to do so and half the time the teachers forgot I should be wearing them. But Mam was in real trouble because the twins grew fast and they had to be dressed alike or all hell was let loose. So it was always two more vests, two more pairs of shoes, two more cardigans. Meanwhile, Betty and I were still growing and too far apart in age to wear each other's clothes. Mam's life became a nightmare of trying to make do. It was obviously not the time to spring on her a demand for fifteen shillings and sixpence to replace glasses I'd lost half on purpose.

I found that by walking halfway home I could save half the bus fare. Taking a bus to Stonegate Circus - actually a roundabout - I could hitch a lift the rest of the way. A very helpful AA man on duty at the Circus would stop cars and vans for me if I was late, and ask them to take me. Consequently I rolled up to Allerton in cars, vans, rubbish lorries - and every lift meant I saved part of the bus fare.

What were the teachers doing while I was riding up the hill? They were in Assembly worshipping God of course, except for the teacher on late duty patrolling the corridors. But she was on the far side of the school - I was never caught arriving late.

*

After my first year at Allerton I was no longer in Upper 3C where I was friendless and isolated. At the end of the school year came exams and for exams you didn't need homework. You needed to swot up the night before, you needed a good memory and a cool head, you needed to read fast and to write very fast indeed. I might have been made for exams. To my own surprise I came top in three subjects, bottom in two and did pretty well in the others. In music, which was all clefs and semiquavers, I distinguished myself by getting the lowest mark ever recorded in an Allerton exam - 9%. The headmistress was so shocked she ordered me to do the music exam over again. The second time I reached a new low - 7%. The only marks I got were for memorising the sol-fa notes of a folk song, and the second time around I'd forgotten some.

*

Now in those days, and for many years to come, we all lived in hope of the Great Transformation Scene. The greatest of all would be the end of the war, we were sure of that, for afterwards everything would be different. No more poverty, injustice, torture, bombings, misery, wounded, broken families, broken lives.

No details existed in our heads as to how this desirable state of affairs would be achieved. The moment the war was won, Fairy Godmother would wave her magic wand. All the lights would shine again - we had a song about that: *When the lights go on again, All over the world.*

In this glittering scenario, peace would be the end of all our troubles. The dried eggs in tins would suddenly become real eggs in the cupboard, ration books would be burnt in victory bonfires, skies would be blue forever - another song explained that - fields would be green, larks would sing ceaselessly in the sky and nightingales appear in Berkeley Square. Toothache, old age and death would disappear, abolished by the wonders of modern science which could achieve absolutely anything. I was convinced that by the time I grew up science would have found the answer to death, and undaunted by the prospect of eternal life, I started to worry about people in the future spying on me.

Time travellers bored silly with their own people, with nothing better to do would gather around time-telescopes to watch me pick my nose. And it was no use telling myself that they couldn't possibly be watching me all the time. I had such a guilty conscience about so many of my activities that I couldn't get the vision of these snotty-nosed interlopers out of my head. I had started to read science fiction from a stall in Leeds market; sci-fi had not yet reached the libraries. It was deemed rather disreputable reading and existed only in magazines; not exactly pornography, but not far from it. The magazines were all American and not new, but cheap enough to buy and some of the stories were quite convincing.

But to return to the transformation scene; there was not only The One Great Victory transformation, but many individual transformations. Girls especially were brought up to trust in magical solutions for any problem. Starting with Cinderella and the Sleeping Beauty, we learned the *Some-day-my-Prince-will-come* Syndrome, which was then reinforced by stories in *Woman*, *Woman's Own* and, the soppiest of the lot, the *Woman's Weekly*.

Week after week we read stories about very ordinary girls with sallow skins and mousy hair, girls lacking in personality but inevitably fond, nay devoted, to their aged mothers, invalid fathers, tiny brothers and dogs and cats. Inevitably along would come a handsome rich bachelor, worldly-wise and sickened by the cynical antics of the predatory females who surrounded him, and bang! she would end up with her face in his hands. Her face, mind you, no other part of her anatomy, while he brokenly murmured words of slavery. From secretary to boss's wife, from nurse to Mrs Head Surgeon of the Cottage Hospital, all in one simple step.

However, the editors of these magazines knew that not all women were willing to sit around knitting and waiting for their Prince to come. A second type of transformation was provided for those more energetic. This relied on the theme that any man who constantly behaved as if he hated you was actually madly in love with you. The transformation came at the story's end, where once again, taking your face into his hands, he would brokenly confess the truth. He had only acted like a loathsome bully because he was trying to fight his love for you. This transformation was male rather than female, Demon King became Prince Charming. God knows how many poor women with bullying bosses and bruising husbands became totally confused. It never occurred to us that in real life men who do horrible things to you and act as if they hate you are very likely to hate you and be horrible.

For all its readers the women's mag market insisted that if only you bought the right make-up, put it on with the right technique, wore the right clothes - yellow, great on sallow skins - you could win through.

To prove it they took June to a famous hairdresser who sneered at her awful hair, cut one half of it off and re-shaped the other, so that her low forehead became high. Next he'd dye it a different colour that suited her sallow skin. When he'd finished with her he'd toss her on to the make-up expert, always a woman, who shoved on rouge in strategic places so that the double chin was no longer discernible and her cheekbones stood out in all the right places. It was better than plastic surgery. Her mouth was enlarged and glowing with the right shade of lipstick, her eye-shadow in the right places, so she looked all alluring. Thrilled and throbbing with delight, June would then be taken and dressed so that her bosom expanded and her hips decreased.

The camera crew then took photos of the radiant new June - she was always

CITY SQUARE

Since this picture was taken in the 1930s this particular corner has been developed on two occasions. Currently the very nasty, egg box architecture, Norwich Union building of the 1960s is being replaced by a Postmodernist structure.

said to be radiant. Wrapped up in money, smeared over with foundation creme and caked with Max Factor, gooey-eyed with mascara and eye-shadow, smiling at us like a million dollars, there was June. You too, the message implied, could look glamorous and fashionable and radiant.

Accompanying the final photos were always a number of diagrams - the severely scientific element of the article. They showed you how to put on the eye-shadow and the rouge. These diagrams bore the same relationship to reality as my mother's sex booklets did to sex. They might have been accurate but they did not help a beginner to know what to do.

We studied these transformations carefully, and from time to time it seemed to me that the latest candidate had been better off before they began their magic. Sometimes it was clear that the new hairdo would not survive two minutes in the open air. But on the whole all this propaganda had its effect, and was reinforced by the Mills and Boon novels, many of which specialised in transformation scenes. Hence I was prepared for a transformation in my own life, but no book, story or magazine had ever mentioned the one that happened to me.

One day when the twins were about three, I took them to town on a Saturday afternoon. We went into Lewis's to spend some pocket-money. They were arguing at a counter over what to buy. I gave them good advice and they ignored it. The counter assistant decided to intervene on my behalf.

"You ought to listen to your mother," she said sternly.

She meant me. I was all of thirteen years old.

The twins paid no attention and went on arguing.

"I'm not their mother, I'm their sister," I protested.

She didn't bother to argue. She gave me one swift disbelieving glance.

I was amazed.

For weeks I tried to convince myself that this was one stupid shop assistant. I might have succeeded if I hadn't taken the twins to Lyons tea-shop, just as Mam had taken me.

Now during the war the tea-shop had been turned into a self-service cafeteria, but you could get gooey fake cream-cakes there, and all the paraphernalia of carpets and mirrors remained in place. It was very popular and there were no seats left on the ground floor, so we had to go upstairs. Carrying the tray and thinking of nothing in particular, I looked into one of the huge mirrors and saw a pleasant-looking young matron, obviously a mother, with two very pretty little girls in tow.

That mother was me.

I don't know how, but years of my childhood disappeared down the drain at that moment.

*

In Harehills at least half the women believed in the Evil Eye, and Mam was one of them. They refused to credit the existence of germs, bacteria and viruses. It was their conviction that kids got ill because someone put the Evil Eye on them, ill-wished them; that was enough.

Their logic was inscrutable. Once the child fell ill due to the Evil Eye, you didn't take him/her to the nearest witch doctor to be un-magicked. No, you went to a proper doctor or Leeds Infirmary, to be dealt with by modern science. But you spent ages brooding on the problem of who had done it.

Now Benson Street was such a thoroughly unhealthy place that even the most gormless Jewish mother - and mine was far from gormless - realised why I got whooping cough, diphtheria, jaundice. Betty's illnesses caused no supernatural maundering because she'd been ill from the word Go. It was clearly useless to blame the neighbours for Betty's ailments, but the twins were a different matter. To my horror Mam would solemnly ponder on who had put the Evil Eye on them if they caught something eminently catchable such as a common cold. She'd say, "That Mrs Something looked at them in a very funny way...said she'd never seen such pretty girls...must be jealous..."

She brooded over the problem and I mean that. She'd sit with her head down, muttering. When I raved at her as illogical, primitive, next door to crazy, she went on, "Shut up, you. You know nothing about it. It couldn't have been Mrs Baker, she likes them. Leave me alone, I'm studying who it could be." That was the word she used, studying.

Though we made fun of this for years afterwards it was not funny then. The truth is I was frightened. How could she say such things and believe them, and refuse to listen to my logical explanations? I didn't know what to do. Luckily Mam was cured not by my preaching biology and logic but by the self-same neighbours who believed in the Evil Eye.

Now Betty didn't look like a witch but I must admit she was elfin. Her pointed chin, huge blue eyes, sharp nose and thin little body set her off from all the other kids in our street. She was also an outspoken critic of babies; she had her reasons. Being clever she wrapped up her dislike of babies in a speech which she often delivered. It went like this, "It's just that all new babies are quite ugly. Later on they can get to be very beautiful but for the first few months they just look red and funny and not a bit attractive."

So when a fairly new baby was taken out in its pram for the first time and Betty was invited to admire it, she gave her speech. The baby's mother was not amused and when it took sick a couple of days later she remembered what Betty had said. She told all the other mothers that Betty had put the Evil Eye on her baby. A crowd gathered outside our house.

My mother went out to meet them. I went too, to give her moral support.

She didn't need it.

Mam came from a family whose women had "wiped the floor" with a long line of factory managers and workshop owners. Everything I'd ever called her she called them back with knobs on. All the arguments I'd used against her she used against them, with style and vim and vigour. "You ought to be ashamed of yourselves," was the essence of her conclusion. "Go home and thank God you're not even sillier than you are, accusing a little girl of three of making your baby ill! Pray God to forgive you, you daft lot of spiteful bitches. Idiots. Lumps! Evil Eye, what a load of barmy rot! Go home!"

And home they went. Shamefaced and muttering, they went home.

Mam and I went back into the house to congratulate ourselves, but when I looked at my face in the kitchen comb-box mirror, I was dead white. I could hardly recognise myself.

*

Other girls at school had carpets on the living-room floor but we had lino in brown and white squares. Every Thursday night Mam went into a frenzy of cleaning and imposed a part on me: scrubbing the floors. First I had to boil a kettle of water to take the chill off, mix it with cold, then sweep the floor, scrub it till the white squares were really white, then wipe it dry with the floor cloth. There were no detergents, only soap, and I worked on my hands and knees patch by patch. Getting it absolutely dry was essential and the hardest part of the proceedings.

Thursday night was always a misery, wringing the floorcloth dry time after time.

But why Thursday night? It didn't make sense to me. Why this night and no other?

Then I read that Russian housewives believed that the goddess Freya, whose name gives us Friday, visited every house on Friday. Consequently they cleaned up on Thursday to be ready for the visit. The mystery was solved. I, Gloria Benjamin of 8 Hares Terrace Leeds 8, was taking part in a ritual designed to appease a Russian goddess. I felt relieved. At least this was better than suspecting my mother was barmy.

Years later in Israel I learned that all Jewish housewives clean up on a Thursday because the Sabbath arrives at sunset on Friday. If I'd been told I was preparing the house for the visit of the Sabbath Angel, I might have enjoyed it more. Then again, perhaps not.

Washing up was the real horror. I had to wash up every night at least, though Mam coped with umpteen washings-up during the day. You had to begin by clearing the table and waging a campaign against Mam who threw gobs of fat and potato peelings into the sink. I couldn't cure her. While she was cooking she threw all the spare bits and pieces into the sink - onion skins, fish heads, the lot. By the time I started operations it was always full of cold water with solidified grease floating on top and assorted muck underneath. With my bare hands I had to fish out all the scraps - some slimy - and empty the sink to put the washing up bowl in place. Then I needed two kettles of boiling water.

This entailed a serious problem.

Kettle number one was easy enough, but mixed with cold it took me only half way through the washing up. The moment I emptied kettle number one it had to be refilled for kettle number two whilst it was still hot and steamy. Since I'd been scalded a couple of times when I tried to lift the lid, I'd fill the second kettle from the spout. And if Dad was around he went berserk.

If Dad caught me performing this verboten act, he hit me so hard across the face I went staggering against the kitchen wall. I don't know why. He was not deliberately cruel on other occasions, he just behaved this way whenever I filled the kettle from the spout or used the same knife for the butter and jam. There is no guessing what triggered the violence.

Naturally I took precautions. Before refilling the kettle I'd look round to make

sure he wasn't there. For years and years after I left home, hundreds of miles away from Hares Terrace, I'd look around before I put the spout of a kettle beneath a tap.

At such times I did not love my father. It's also worth noting that when he was stationed away from home I wasted no time worrying about him. His survival I took for granted; he was like Mam, immortal. He thought so too. Once when he was home between postings the air-raid siren wailed in the middle of the night. Mam got dressed, dressed the twins and begged him to come with us to the shelter. He refused to budge. She had us outside at the front gate and yelled at him, "Jimmy Benjamin! Come to the shelter!"

He hung half out of the bedroom window and yelled back, "If the buggers come, let the buggers come! I'm not going anywhere."

Then he disappeared inside. He just went back to bed. "If it's got your name on it, it's got your name on it," he used to say philosophically.

We went on to the shelter. That night a shell fell through the roof of Number 4, only one house away. It merely confirmed Dad's view of the universe.

But men had adventurous lives, they weren't stuck with household duties. We were at home doing the mangling every wash day. The mangle was a large object dominating the kitchen. It served as a table except on washing day.

Then Mam did something to it, the top went backwards and it was no longer a table. Two large long white rubber rollers appeared. In the days before washing machines and spin dryers, you put sheets and towels through the mangle to get rid of the surplus water before you hung them out to dry.

You needed two people to operate the mangle successfully, one to turn the handle and guide the sopping wet sheet through the rollers, the other to guide the emerging sheet so that it fell neatly, folding itself into the clothes basket instead of draping itself all over the floor. I helped by doing the guiding as it took Mam's strength to turn the handle. After finishing, you still had to empty the zinc bathtub of water - it streamed down the mangle as you fed the sheets into it - and wipe down the rollers and make it a table again.

This monstrosity was in fact a labour-saving device. Without the mangle you'd be trying to hang out dripping sheets with an icy wind blowing the drip into your face. Everything else such as slips and knickers had to be wrung out by hand, unless the great machine was ready for its task.

Crumbs were the enemy, for every slice of bread you cut scattered about 200

BOAR LANE 1940

Anyone looking above the first level will recognise that the main architectural features of the street have changed little since it was widened in the 1860s. There is a great deal of solid building in the Renaissance and Gothic styles, especially on the railway station side.

The function of Boar Lane has changed considerably. Sixty years ago this was a street of fashionable eating houses.

In 1933, before trams had been superseded by buses, a fleet of 476 ran over 124 miles of track.

crumbs in all directions. You couldn't help creating crumbs and more crumbs. Toasters didn't exist for working-class people. To obtain toast, you cut a slice of bread, carried it crumbily into the living room and stuck it on the end of a toasting fork. Then you knelt in front of the fire and tried to concentrate. If you didn't there'd be a familiar burning smell and you'd spend the next three minutes scraping burnt bits off your bread. Experts left the toast on the fork until it was brown but before it began to burn. We kids had no expertise. We would keep examining the toast to see if it was ready and in the process it dropped off the fork and into the fire. Few pieces of toast got done without drama. You could end up with a piece half-charred on one side, half raw on the other.

The crumbs created by toast mixed with the wood shavings from Dad's trousers and both were tackled with sweeping brush and dustpan. No vacuum cleaners in those days. Yet no matter how often we swept the floor, or how severely we swept, it was never quite free of crumbs and wood shavings.

This would be a problem now, but then community attitudes were firmly in favour of dirt. "You've got to eat a peck a muck before you die," was a Yorkshire saying, always flung at us when we protested that something we had to eat was dirty. Insecticides and pesticides hardly existed, so we were always finding worms in apples and snails in lettuces.

Kippers' eyes fascinated me. In the middle of every kipper's eye there is a tiny golden ball, perfectly round, opaque yet translucent. All fish were bought whole from Leeds Market and many's the hour I spent watching Mam scrape off the scales and slice open the belly to gut the fish. Fish were easy compared to hens; they had to be scalded, scraped, disembowelled, taking particular care not to pierce the dark green object which was the gall bladder. The grain pouch was emptied, cleaned, stuffed with "helzel" sewed up securely and shoved back inside. A merry time we had of it!

I sometimes wonder if today's girls get anorexia nervosa because they've never had to do any real housework. How could you be totally obsessed with your own body after watching a chook being dismembered and cooked?

Coal was another source of drama. How is it that writers have managed to produce entire novels about coal miners without even one scene depicting a row about coal? Everybody argued and fought over it. Coal was not magically transported into your living room and delivered onto the flames, it was kept either downstairs in the cellar or outside in the coal shed, and for eight months in the year, somebody had to shovel the coal into a bucket, carry the bucket into the living room and eventually feed the fire.

Our coal was outside in a little shed and outside it might be raining. You'd scrabble away at the coal face while the rain dripped onto you. If it was snowing, and it snowed often in winter, the snow melted on you. If it was windy, the wind whipped your hair into your face. Sometimes it would be rainy and windy in which case you'd get a faceful of wet freezing hair. Sometimes the coal man had just been so when you opened the shed door a load of coal fell out on you. At other times the shed was nearly empty because he hadn't been and that was worse because only a few lumps were left at the far end and that meant you had to crawl right into it. You left looking like a chimney sweep.

Our family practice on a winter's evening was to sit around the fire secretly calculating the chances of being told to fetch the next scuttle of coal. Whose turn was it? Who was trying to get out of her turn? How long could we put off going for the coal without the fire going out? But when a good fire got going it was wonderful.

A coal fire isn't like any other fire. As it burns, the coal releases tiny spurts of gas that hiss and bubble and glow blue, set off by orange flames. A coal fire is always changing. It leaps and dances, sputters then radiates itself to embers and ashes. You can poke it with a poker and the grey ashes glow red again, add more coal and the leaping flames return. I read in poems that some see pictures in the flames. I never saw anything but flames, fire and coal - and for me that was enough.

When I was about eighteen the coal fire was replaced by a gas heater, and I was stricken. You can't poke a gas heater, sieve through its ashes, burn love-letters in the flames. On the other hand you can't throw rubbish in it either.

Every evening Mam would come in from the kitchen holding a mass of muck from the sink-strainer - muck tastefully wrapped in newspaper but seeping with tea-leaves and grease. Squash and splash, straight into the fire despite "Oh Mam!"

"It'll burn through," she'd say grimly.

And so it did, eventually. On the way it stank and reeked and took all heat away from the fire, but there was only one rubbish collection per week in one rubbish bin per house, and convenience foods didn't exist. She had no choice.

*

When I was about thirteen the family stepped up their war on education. For my thirteenth birthday I was bought the following presents: a lipstick and a Max Factor compact filled with face powder, and urged in no uncertain terms to use them. Dad also sent me to town with money and orders to buy - no kidding - a pair of high-heeled shoes.

"You're a big girl now," he said.

I would willingly have bought high heels to please him, if I'd found a pair that could fit. Alas, my stubby toes and broad chubby feet - left foot even broader than the right - defeated their plans for my future. I came home with a pair of eminently sensible shoes, shoes I could walk the miles home in happily, but no good for dancing. Dad was obviously disappointed and sulky about it. "I thought I told you to get high heels!"

"But they don't fit me - I can't walk in them!"

"You ought to go dancing at the Jewish Youth Club."

I was baffled. I didn't like dancing.

There was a Jewish Youth Club at Moortown Corner and the bane of my life was a girl called Maureen, a neighbour who went there. This paragon of virtue left school obligingly at fourteen, took a job in an office, earned money to buy herself smart clothes and nylons, and got herself engaged and married quick smart. If I left school at fourteen, I too could keep myself, earn money for clothes, get engaged, get married and get myself off my parents' hands. If!

If I lost weight, if I wore high heels, if I went dancing on Saturday nights instead of reading a library book, all this could be mine!

I tried once or twice to go dancing but found I couldn't dance, not really.

Dad took me once to the Jubilee Hall, led me upstairs to the dance floor then disappeared downstairs to enjoy the snooker and booze. At the end of the dance he reappeared to take me home, which was the best part of the evening. In between, I'd have been better off with a good book.

Most of the time I was ignored - so were many other girls. I just stood there with a happy smile pasted on my face, feeling furious.

There were other problems. I had no natural sense of rhythm, so when I was asked to dance by good dancers, they were thankful enough to let me go after one dance and I was grateful to be gone. But there were those much older than me who couldn't dance either. They clod-hopped round the floor holding me too close, pushing their chests against my breasts.

"Do you come here often?"

"Haven't I seen you before somewhere?"

"Nice music isn't it?"

"Good band, don't you think?"

Their hands were sweaty, their breath was bad, there wasn't one I could fancy in a thunderstorm; greasy hair clogged up with Brylcream, pimples, dandruff, stupidity, lechery. I should have kicked the ankles of quite a few, but in those days I was too timid to attack grownups no matter how disgustingly they acted. Often on the tram or in the cinema a stranger would rove his hands all over me. It took me years to develop a quick jab of the elbow that made groping fingers recoil in split seconds.

All this I did not explain to my parents, because they never asked me. Not once. They took it for granted that every normal, healthy, red-blooded girl enjoyed dancing on a Saturday night. Sally and Hetty loved it. Mam herself had a natural sense of rhythm. Why couldn't I be normal?

Throughout the years I've had to accept the fact that I became a fiasco to my parents. They loved me but they did not like me. I was no good for them. They wanted me to be somebody else, somebody I did not want to be.

Together with the dance-and-get-married propaganda went the warnings: "Educated girls don't get married. Boys don't like educated girls. It's all right to go to night school and learn shorthand and typing. Then you can be a secretary - nine to five, office hours, good money. But not Oxford, not university. Secretaries have plenty of money to buy pretty clothes. You could marry a Nice Yiddishe Boy."

They intensified this rubbish when I was thirteen because fourteen was the legal age for leaving school and jobs were plentiful. Also, if I got work and brought home my wages, they could try again for a boy. They would have forced me out of high school openly if they'd dared, if I hadn't been so vociferous, loudmouthed, angry.

I was hurt. And bewildered.

What was all this stuff about getting married?

Why was it supposed to be so marvellous?

What happened when you got married? This: you ended up begging your husband to let you have an extra half-crown because the twins needed vests. You stayed home, he went to the pub. You nagged him for two years before he fixed the garden fence. You whinged day and night that you could have married the boss's son. He wouldn't change his dirty socks.

You had babies. Wonderful, marvellous. I knew about babies. But they didn't even stay babies, they grew up.

Our street was filled with married couples. Being married didn't make them happy, not so's you'd notice. Only Addie and Victor, who kissed in the kitchen, were tolerably pleased with life. Mam and Dad were always rowing. Married life, to listen to Mam, was one long suffer-suffer. Yes, they had their happy half hours - "we have no money but we do see life!" she'd say, with a bitter laugh.

So what she said to me in words was not the true message she gave out. At one level it was, "If you are fat and educated, you'll never get married."

Translated - and I translated it - her message went like this, "If you stay fat and get educated, you'll escape being married," or in one word, more simply, "Escape!"

She didn't mean to tell me this consciously. She would have sworn she was trying to teach me the facts of life. Unfortunately I learned from the music as well as the words.

*

When I was eleven my periods started. I felt ill and went to bed. There was a slow dragging pain in my guts and blood between my legs. When I saw the blood, I knew what was happening. Mam came into the bedroom and I said, "I've got my first period!"

Now according to Evelyn Home and my psychology books, this was a wonderful moment, a sign that you were now entering womanhood, a cause for rejoicing. I waited for words of joy. What I got was a very embarrassed, "I suppose you know all about it."

I said with a sinking feeling, "Yes, you don't have to explain it to me, I've read all the books."

"Oh good." She was very relieved.

UPPER BRIGGATE 1930

Rothwell's, the mock Tudor quality furnishing store in the background, has been destroyed but the buildings in the centre still stand. In the 1930s Parkers was a Temperance Hotel. The most important building in this street stands opposite. The Grand Theatre, built in 1878, originally seated 2600 people.

"But it hurts. I feel awful."

"I'll get you something." She went downstairs and brought back a hot drink - not tea or cocoa.

"What's this?"

"Drink it, it'll do you good."

She had mixed gin, hot water and sugar. It must have been the family remedy. I drank it and was violently sick. Then I went on retching, rushing to the loo with diarrhoea and sicking up again. This continued for six hours and left me feeling that a horse had kicked me in the stomach.

For the next forty years or so this revolting scene was enacted monthly. In time I discovered that my only allergy was alcohol at this time of the month. Nothing stopped the pain, the vomiting and diarrhoea, but alcohol in any form was guaranteed to make it worse.

From that month on I had to buy my own sanitary towels, a dreaded duty. These things slotted into an elastic harness called a sanitary belt, and they were supposed to absorb all the blood. Getting them and getting rid of them once they'd been used were ghastly tasks.

At the end of the next street was a chemist - a male chemist. Occasionally his wife was at the counter, a cause for some relief but not total.

Both of them were adept at keeping their faces absolutely expressionless. You waited till the shop emptied, then put your money on the counter and said in a low, strained tone, "A packet of sanitary towels please."

Without a word they'd fish out the packet from behind the counter and cover it with a plain brown paper bag. The theory behind this was that once the packet was covered up, no one would know what it was. But the bag's shape was easy to identify. It was clear to me that people could tell. Deeply ashamed, I'd run for home as fast as menstrual cramps would let me.

Soon I discovered that even so-called super-absorbent sanitary towels weren't enough. They had to be backed up with a thick layer of cotton wool or the blood soaked through everything. Oh the joys of womanhood, the lies of Evelyn Home!

That was only the beginning; you had to keep changing the damn things so you could bleed through the next one, then they were wrapped up in paper and burnt. But not in front of the family, not with the other rubbish, not in front of your father - God forbid he should see your used s-t's. Incineration was achieved by waiting until he and the fire were out. Then you mucked around with newspaper and matches till they burned, and since they were sodden with blood they often wouldn't. Sometimes they started to burn and stopped, and you didn't know it. Dad would come to make up the fire and he'd find the grate full of half-charred s-t's. What was I supposed to do? A few things like s-t's were awarded paper bags but not many. Newspapers were kept down to four pages and we had one newspaper per day. Newspapers were used for starting the fire and wrapping up the real rubbish, not sanitary towels. And there were no plastic bags at all, they hadn't been invented.

I did find out that sugar will start a fire, but sugar was rationed. Enough of this. Suffice it to say that womanhood is not what it's cracked up to be.

At Allerton I was the first in my class to develop proper breasts, though I was also the youngest. After gym and games, in the shower, everyone stared at me. There was no dirty talk at that stage. I didn't know the words "tit" and "boobs" wasn't in English. I had breasts - babies got the titty, and it wasn't the same thing.

And to cover my breasts, the cheapest nastiest towel in class. It was never taken home to be washed because I could just imagine Mam's reaction. "Oh so now I've got to wash your towel every week, have I ? Washing the twins' nappies isn't enough, is it? Well Lady Godiva, you're the one who wanted to go to High School and be a lady."

When my periods came a couple of unlucky girls shared my fate. You couldn't have a shower if you had your period. You shouldn't wash your hair either. Why? God knows. You would catch a cold, get pneumonia, your hair might fall out and leave you bald. You waited until the others were in the showers then sidled up to the gym teacher, who stood at the entrance marking off your name in a little black book. Then you said, in a hushed whisper, "Miss Wilmott, please may I be excused from taking a shower because I've got my period. "

She looked at you sharply and made a note in her book. Rumour had it that she counted the weeks - so nobody could get out of having a shower more than once a month. Playing hookey saved me from many a shower.

Meanwhile my breasts went on growing without benefit of bra - Mam was busy with Betty and the twins - so they got heavy, drooped, and by the time she noticed this no shop bra would fit me. There was little choice in wartime. So she hauled me off to her own Jewish bra-maker, a woman used to fulsome figures. Muttering about puppy-fat they squeezed me into two custom-built cups made of strong pink cotton and elastic, designed on engineering principles. That woman could have built the Solway Bridge. Once in her bras, a girl was safe. No snapping a hook and eye, for there were rows of hooks and eyes, ten pairs. Just as well too. Men were impressed by my large breasts, and the type most impressed were lecherous louts I longed to thump. But my bras were another expense for the family. Oh, if only I would get myself a job, wear lipstick and make-up.

Mrs Baker from up the street often reported me if I went to town without make-up. "Saw your Gloria in Briggate on Saturday, not wearing a trace of lipstick. And she's a big girl now, isn't she?"

Once she even managed to tattle on me before I got home. Mam was waiting for me at the back door - which was next to the kitchen sink. "What were you doing in town without your make-up? Mrs Baker says she saw you in Briggate without any lipstick! You're a big girl now..."

I was supposed to make sense of this when most of the other girls in my class were strictly forbidden to wear make-up, and longed to.

*

Forget it Mam, there was no hope at all of extracting me from high school and putting me into an office because I was no longer in Upper 3C where I had no friends. I'd been moved to the "A" stream where the girls were more intelligent, and I was in love with Valerie Wylie.

Well, I had a crush on her and wrote soppy poetry about her. She had flair, she had style, she had a middle class upbringing.

From Valerie and her friends I learned about life in the middle class and boy! It was awful. The more I learned the more horrified I was, and the more I pitied them. But the more they learnt about my life, the more horrified they were, the more they pitied me. Our horror, our pity were equally sincere.

"A lady should never leave the house without wearing gloves" said Valerie on our long walks home.

Fancy that! All these years I'd lived in Hares Terrace rushing in and out at the drop of a hat, never wearing gloves.

Mam let me listen to *Saturday Night Theatre* on the radio till the bitter end, even the play was by George Bernard Shaw. "My mother wouldn't let me listen to anything like that," said Margaret Addison virtuously. Middle class parents controlled every facet of their children's lives. They couldn't just go to the bread-bin and take a slice of bread and put jam on it, or pick up an orange or apple as they passed the fruit bowl. They had to sit down at set times and keep their elbows off the table. Their reading and listening were strictly censored. They were sent to bed at bedtime like babies, in the middle of *Saturday Night Theatre*. If the play was interesting, Mam would never have done that to me - she'd be listening too.

In that "A" stream class consisting of thirty-two girls, there were ten called "Margaret" because Princess Margaret had been born that year - and I was the only girl without a room of her own. I was also the only one who got half a crown pocket money on a Saturday morning; the others got less. I was the only girl who could take a tram into town alone, go to whatever film I pleased and plaster my face with any mixture of powder and paint I desired.

Not one of them had younger brothers or sisters.

Not one of them was sent out to play in the street when it was raining, with the firm adjuration, "Get out of the house!"

"But it's raining!"

"That's all right, you're not made of sugar and you won't melt in the rain."

If middle-class girls were naughty - there's no other word for it, naughty is correct - they were sent to bed without any supper. My mother would regard this as child abuse and so would I. Hitting was one thing, starvation was another. I showed them my bruised legs and they were appalled.

"You're not being brought up," said Addi, "you're being dragged up. I told my mother about you and that's what she said."

I was furious. I got my revenge by explaining to Addie that she was really in love with her own father. She'd never heard of the Oedipus complex and in a spate of pure spite I reduced her to tears. "You really want to marry him and take him away from your mother," I explained kindly.

"I don't! I don't!" she wept. I went on explaining. After that day she did not mention my upbringing again.

I fell in love with Valerie Wylie because she was the tomboy rebel of the class. One day when I'd come early to do some copying she followed me in, perched on

the radiator opposite the door and as the other girls entered, insulted each and every one of them. She did it without rhyme, reason or warning. It was marvellous. She was marvellous, totally vivid and alive.

I loved her just as she was and wanted only to walk home with her while she talked. This boon was granted me. We never so much as held hands yet I wrote a book of poems about her and the cherry tree in her garden.

> *The dawn-flushed petals are your skin*
> *Your eyes the diamond dew within.*
> *Your every smile recalls to me*
> *The blossom on your cherry tree.*

That's all I really remember; my love for her was perfect, complete, like my love for Adam. No regrets. Yet sometimes I felt an unwonted awareness: "This is the last time I shall ever love like this, without wanting anything in exchange. This is the last time I shall simply love."

Betty read my poems and admired them - even learned some by heart. She can still recite one of my songs to Valerie. "Your eyes would shame those azure skies, my love, and perfume lives forever in your hair."

Tosh. Why did I write such claptrap? Because I thought that was what a love-song ought to sound like, not because I cared tuppence about the azure or otherwise of her eyes. Her hair smelled of nothing in particular. I knew very well that she was not beautiful. There was a truly lovely girl in our class called Heather Nicholson; such girls are strange rarities, yet out of seven hundred and fifty Allerton girls, Valerie had a quality that stopped my eyes. I could have stared at her for hours and did. Heather's beauty was distinct from her personality. As a person she was pleasant, kind, intelligent, friendly. Valerie was different. She had short straight brown hair, pink cheeks and dancing blue eyes.

I can still remember her face. I who can't remember anyone's face, can see Valerie Wylie standing by her garden gate with the cherry tree behind her in full blossom. Her eyes, never still for a moment, are the clue to my memory. She'd stand chatting by the gate, not wanting to invite me in, not able to tear herself away. The pleasure of her company was enough to delight me, I didn't need to be invited inside.

Once when snow was deep we walked home through the fields, laughing and

HAREHILLS 1938

Times were getting more prosperous and a better variety of shops were appearing on the outskirts of the city centre. Linked by tram lines, areas such as this benefited from the prosperity which immediately proceeded the war.

shouting and shrieking with joy. We ate handfuls of snow, drank it, threw it, tramped through snowdrifts. We were delirious with pure joy.

And I was expected to exchange all this for marriage!

*

Now everyone, nieces and nephews and sisters, friends and husbands of friends - I beg your pardon, I know you mean well but please stop trying to adjust this document. I live my life according to my memories, not yours. I made my mistakes and rejoiced and grieved because that's the way it was for me. If I got Sean Watson mixed up with his brother Roy, and forgot the second-hand sewing-machine in the kitchen, or claimed the twins were three when they were actually two and a half, what of it?

I can see I should have stated from the first why I'm writing this book, if it is a book. I think of it as a document.

My Auntie Sadie's lifelong hobby was buying hats. She would spend hours trying on hats, choose one, bring it home and try it on again. At home in the sideboard mirror, it never looked the same. She'd tilt it every which way, then say sadly, "I'm very disappointed in this 'at."

So she would take it back and change it for another, equally unbecoming. Or she would give it away to a friend. Once she said to me, seriously, "I'm very disappointed in my life, I am," in exactly the same tone as the one she used for hat disposal.

Now I feel exactly the opposite.

What I feel about my life is amazement. I am amazed that this is me. Pleased, delighted, sometimes angry and regretful too, but more amazed than anything else. And I want the rest of the world to know about it. I reckon all those people who take me for granted ought to know how amazing my life has been, and if you don't know the past you can't appreciate the present.

The memories are slowly churned into words, the words are typed onto a sheet of paper and come out in a straight line. But my life was not lived in a straight line. My feelings about my family were as many-layered as an onion, and still are. For example, I have told the truth about Dad hitting me with dowel sticks, and my furious reaction. I hated him for it. But in comparison with the girls at school I felt a smug sense of superiority - they did not get hit, they were dealt with in more rational ways that ensured the loss of their freedom. I was tough and they were a namby-pamby lot, totally captive.

As for my family, it was my privilege to call Dad a sadistic brute, Mam a primitive idiot, Betty a moaner, the twins nuisances. My meeting with Mathilde Strassman exposed a deeper layer of truth.

Matty was a Belgian girl of my age whose father had been deported and killed; her mother managed to get them both out of Belgium to stay with cousins in Leeds. She was never in my class but we skulked together in the games pavilion, united in our contempt for hockey and netball. Together we discovered a sort of cellar under the stage in the big assembly hall; it was used as storage space for the school's amateur theatricals. Once down there - it was technically out of bounds - no teachers or prefects would bother us.

Matty was very intelligent, very slender and Jewish. Her nose was long and stuck out like a parrot's beak. She told me about her life; once in England, her mother had dumped her with the cousins, who lived in Sheepscar, and joined the army. Her cousins didn't want her but they could hardly refuse to keep her. Since they were middle-aged and living in a one-bedroom house, they'd rented a room for Matty across the street. She took me there. I was impressed and depressed more than words can say.

The room was appalling. It was just bare wooden boards and a bed and a chair, bare walls with a bare light bulb and a couple of blankets on the bed. Heating was a small one-bar radiator which scarcely took the chill from the air. Then I met the cousins; they were appalling too. Dry and faded, no juice there. No warmth, nothing to take the chill out of her life. Brimming with pity for Matty, I invited her home. She gladly accepted.

I told Mam all about Matty's misery alone in that dreadful room, and she cooked a special meal. Matty sat by the lovely warm fire while the radio played, Mam talked, the twinnies crawled all over her - they loved crawling over visitors - Betty wept and argued and accused the twins, and everyone shrieked in turn. It was a house where no one heard you unless you shouted or screamed. Everyday conversation was carried on like scenes from a Victorian melodrama, Mam said everything three times in a kind of rhythm, and yells were exchanged between the bathroom, kitchen and living-room. A ritual question-and-answer routine between

Mam and me had reached the point where we did not wait for the other to finish her lines but concentrated on our own parts. So we'd be shrieking simultaneously from different rooms, and finding a pair of socks had developed into grand opera without music.

It went like this:

Me: "Where's my socks? Who's taken my socks? I bet those twins have been at my things again. Mam why do you let them mess about with my socks? Why doesn't Dad put a lock on my cupboard so they can't mess about with my things? How many times have I asked you to..."

Mam: "Look in the top drawer! Look in the top drawer! I found them on the floor and I put them in the top drawer! Why d'you always fling your things around and expect me to pick them up and put them away for you? If I've told you once, I've told you a thousand times. Don't fling your things..."

Twins: "It's not us! We get blamed for everything in this house and we don't do anything! Ask Betty if you want to know where your socks are. Go on, ask her! Just because she's crying, you think she didn't take them! Well you ought to know she took your headscarf last week, yes she did!"

Betty: "I didn't, I didn't! They're telling lies! I never touched your headscarf! I never went near your socks! Why do the twins hate me and tell lies about me?" And on and on and on.

Then I'd find the socks, either in the top drawer as Mam had said, or the middle drawer. That the whole to-do was bizarre and completely unnecessary never occurred to us. We all enjoyed the noise and took it for granted that it was right and proper.

Matty sat through all this for a few hours. She spoke very little and I assumed she was overcome with happiness at being in a warm, friendly family circle. I deemed it my duty to see her to the end of the street when she left, and I was glowing with quiet pride. "Well," I said at the corner of Shepherds Lane, "what did you think of them?"

She turned to me a face of frozen horror.

"My God," she said, "I don't know how you stand it."

THE CAST COLLECTION, LEEDS ART GALLERY 1911

George Birkett, an early Art Gallery curator, built a magnificent collection of classical casts which were displayed in the city's Sculpture Gallery. This is where the young Henry Moore saw examples of classical sculpture.

*

From the time the twins were born, Mam was in deep trouble. In those days abortion was totally illegal, though this was no problem for the rich. There were private clinics where for a price - an extremely high price - doctors would certify that they were operating because the patient's life was in danger from the pregnancy. A common trick was to bill the abortion as a D&C - if the patient turned out to be unexpectedly pregnant, that was their "surprise".

In our street every house held a married couple with one or two children. There was no access to private clinics with safe abortions though the women knew backstreet abortionists who operated in the kitchen with unsterile instruments. These too were expensive, so the prevailing method was do-it-yourself.

I hardly know how to begin, so I'll start with simple arithmetic. In our house six people were living on one man's wages. Nobody else in the street had four kids, only the Benjamins. All the mothers were equally determined to avoid "having another" - the word "baby" was never spoken. By the time I was ten I knew that at all costs Mam had to avoid having another.

The things I heard were not overhead but were spoken clearly.

The moment a woman in our street fell pregnant, she started a round of actions designed to abort the foetus; a bottle of gin, a scalding hot bath, followed by redecorating a room. To cause a "miss" Mam worked frenziedly; she moved ladders, climbed up and down ladders, heaved bucketfuls of water and gallons of paint all over the place. If that didn't succeed, there were always coat-hangers and knitting needles.

As far as I know all Hares Terrace did the same, so it baffled me to discover that the City Of Leeds councillors had erected a birth control clinic bang in the middle of town. As the tram on Route No3 swung round the bend into Briggate, I could read the plaque which said:

> *Venereal Diseases Clinic Open Daily* and next to it:
> *City of Leeds Birth Control Clinic 9 a.m.-5 p.m. Mon-Fri.*

Once it dawned on me that there was no need for Mam to mutter about putting her head in the gas oven if she had to have another, I tried to argue with her logically. "Why can't you go to the Birth Control Clinic?"

Her response was fierce and prompt.

"Oh shut up you. You know nothing about it. I can't go there."

Then she'd start again. "I'll kill myself. I'd rather kill myself. Gloria, if I die, promise me you'll look after Betty and the twins."

Terrified, I promised her. I would have promised her anything but I was furious. I wanted to say, "Look after your own bloody children, I want to live my own life," but I didn't dare. Besides I thought she was raving mad.

Again and again I asked her why she didn't go to the Birth Control Clinic. Eventually she answered, "Because I can't stand messing about with myself, that's why."

"So it's better to jump off stepladders and use knitting needles? Mam, are you crazy? What do you call messing about with yourself?"

"I'm not going there, it's no use."

"You're mad, you are."

She smacked my face, which no doubt made her feel better. And in a way she was right. In spite of all my reading I knew nothing about the technicalities of birth control, I only knew it existed. I found out the real reason she wouldn't use the Clinic about thirty years later, when I asked her again. This time, in a calm and happy mood, she was able to tell me.

"Why do you think your Auntie Sally had Jimmy fifteen months after Johnny? Because she went to the Birth Control, and they used to give out Dutch caps, and there were only three sizes, and they didn't fit properly."

Once in Israel I told a friend about the women of Hares Terrace; she was a university lecturer on the history of Jewish migration around the world. She said at once, "You must have come from North Street."

I opened my mouth to say No, when I remembered the name of the huge road at the end of our street in Sheepscar.

"How on earth did you guess? Not North Street itself, but next to it."

"It's easy. There were three main streams of Jewish migration into Leeds. One lot were educated but very devout - they would have gone ahead and had the children. They settled along Chapeltown Road. There was another group; they were educated but not devout. They would have gone to the Birth Control Centre. They settled in Roundhay. And there was a third group, very poor, with no education, and they'd lost their religion too. They were the North Street Jews. So

the moment you told me about a streetful of women aborting themselves, I knew which group it was. You had to come from North Street."

So there you are.

*

The source of the bitterest quarrels between Dad and Mam, though I didn't know it at the time, was this lack of birth control. Mam could not say to her eldest daughter, "Since I'm not allowed by law to get a safe abortion, and we can't afford even an unsafe illegal abortion, we use the withdrawal method. Every time your father gets drunk and has sex with me, he has no control over withdrawal. And every time I abort myself, I run the risk of death." All this emerged years later, put together like the pieces of a jigsaw puzzle in my childhood, knowledge of abortions wasn't linked in any way to Mam's "hysterical" response to Dad's drinking. If I'd have known at that time, I'd have wanted to kill him.

He was always so happy when he was drunk, so reasonable in comparison with her; never aggressive, always loving and generous. We kids rather hoped he'd come home shicker. It led to umpteen arguments, because whenever Mam started campaigning against the booze, we defended him.

"Leave him alone," we'd plead. "It isn't as if he gets drunk every day of the week! Why can't you let him get drunk and enjoy himself? Oh Mam, leave him be."

But she would not, could not, knowing what she did, leave him alone. Christmas and the New Year was one danger period, August Bank Holiday was another. She would rev herself up for weeks in advance, warning him. "You're not going out on Christmas Eve and coming home drunk!"

"No, certainly not," he teased her wickedly. "Not if you don't like it, my littel darling." He always said "little" in that way. In those days she weighed about thirteen stones.

"Don't mock me, Jimmy Benjamin! I mean what I say. You're not going out on Christmas Eve and coming home drunk!"

"Oh, Mam! Let him get drunk! What harm does it do?"

He knew, and she knew, the answer to our question.

That answer must have hung in the air, unspoken, night after night. Once in

REFERENCE LIBRARY

The Central Library was built in 1884 as part of a splendid municipal building project. The room in which Gloria studied was based on a medieval hall with gallery and dais canopy. Such magnificence caught and held her imagination.

despair she said that the twins should have been named not Greta and Brenda but Tetleys' Light Ale and Tetley's Bitter. A drunken man could not withdraw in time to spill his seed outside the womb. But she could not say that. Sensing that a direct onslaught only alienated us, she would change tack and complain about the expense.

"Robin Goodfellow in the pub, treating every man and his dog, treating the barmaid, don't think I don't know! I've seen what they do. Those barmaids, they fling the change down on purpose into a puddle of beer. And your Dad, the silly idiot, he doesn't want to get his hands wet picking it up. All the men are the same, brainless with booze. 'Keep the change, love,' that's what they say. 'Have a drink on me.' Robin Goodfellow, generous Jimmy, Lord Muck! But when it comes to an extra two bob for the twins' new vests, he's got no money. He can't afford it. 'Money doesn't grow on trees,' he says. No by God it doesn't, not for Mrs Benjamin - only for the barmaids at Sheepscar Working Men's Club. Ask them where the money grows. Go on, ask!"

And we listened and learned.

"'Have a drink on me,' he says to his pals. Four or five or six of them, what does it matter, he's that generous. And does he count the change? do *any* of them *ever* count the change? After four or five pints are they even *able* to count the change? Don't make me laugh." She was in no danger of laughing. "I've seen them myself. Scooping up the change, wouldn't bother to count it, he'd be ashamed to, wouldn't he? You don't count change in front of your mates, because they might think you're mean. God forbid your mates should think that, eh?"

She was right and we knew it. He'd flush up, trying to control himself. "Just scoop up the change, never mind if there's half a crown missing, you wouldn't want your mates to think you're mean! But when the twins need a new pair of shoes, that's a different story. A completely different story. 'Take it out of the housekeeping' he says! Two pairs of shoes, not one, and they've got to have them this week. They've grown out of the others. Are the poor kids to go barefoot because their Dad's the barmaids' best friend? Are we all supposed to starve while you and your mates pour beer down your throats till you're sick with it? You'll have to give me more money, I can't manage on this!" And she'd wave the housekeeping money at him. Even now my heart hurts for her.

And for him too. Betty and I would gladly have given him the right to go out and get drunk every night of the week. Mam's tactics often failed; he'd fling himself out of the house to the more congenial atmosphere of the pub. But sometimes she was really desperate. Twice she packed a huge suitcase that she could hardly lug down the stairs.

"Look after Betty and the twins for me, I'm leaving. I can't take any more. Gloria, promise me you'll look after the twins. You'll have to be a mother to them. I'm going back home, I can't manage any more."

Now I was well used to her histrionics, and Dad even more so, but on these two occasions she meant it. If I was terrified, Dad was appalled. He'd stop her at the door, grab the suitcase, plead with her. It was awful. She'd be screaming, then crying, then letting out dull hopeless sobs. The hopelessness of those sounds was worst of all. By that time she'd be giving in, but at the peak of the quarrel I almost hoped that she'd find the guts to escape.

In the end we'd all go back to bed, and Dad would be careful with the booze for a few months. And I wouldn't know what to feel. Only I learned the technique of taunting Dad as well as the uselessness of it, and this was to cause trouble in the years ahead.

I also learned something more useful: escape. There is always the connection between past and present; the scenes at the kitchen door, that open door, stayed in my memory and chartered the course of my life. The suitcase was packed. She could have gone.

She stayed. Does it matter why she stayed? She loved him, she loved us, she was afraid to leave him; in those days the outlook for deserting wives was bleak indeed. God knows what would have happened to us.

But for years after, I not only refused to get married, I would not even take a job that held me down. My proudest boast was, that I could leave anywhere within twenty-four hours. That I'd be ready to leave, packed up and waiting to go, on a plane to England or anywhere else.

*

When the twins were three, Mam fell pregnant again.

She induced her own abortion. It wasn't called an abortion. They used to call such episodes "misses".

After doing everything she could to cause a miscarriage, she collapsed in the lift at Lewis's. The twins were with her at the time. There was a huge pool of blood underneath her, blood everywhere. Luckily Lewis's was minutes from Leeds Infirmary and the ambulance was in time. Technically she could have been prosecuted for causing the abortion, but it was hard to prove such cases and the authorities turned a blind eye.

Mam was in Leeds Infirmary for three weeks. I wasn't allowed to see her more than once. In those days hospital staff truly enforced visiting hours - not even hours, in fact, but thirty minutes morning and evening. It was considered too upsetting for a child to see its mother in hospital, so Betty wasn't allowed in at all.

During those three weeks the twins were sent to Cowper Street Nursery, all day and every day. It was one of the government nurseries kept open all day because mothers were needed to work in the factories. We tried to explain to the twins that Mam was in hospital and ill, but I don't know how much they understood. They hated and feared the nursery.

Every morning they screamed and screamed. They say today that they were treated so cruelly there that they never got over it. They were beaten, made to eat things they hated and locked up in the dark when they vomited.

Whatever happened, I don't know. I do know that before they went to the nursery they were happy children. After the nursery, they were different They used to be lovely little kids. Dad's teasing didn't have much effect because he wasn't home most of the time. The way they wrapped themselves round strangers in the park was proof that they adored men; they'd coo "Daddy!" and hug anyone, so he hadn't really hurt their hearts.

But after the nursery, they were different.

They were always looking for a reason to whinge. In their eyes they were what Mam called "badly done-to".

"You love her more than you love me," each would whine, meaning the other. I remained exempt from this because they knew very well: I couldn't tell who was which.

Reasonable requests to behave were taken as sheer persecution.

They screamed at everything they didn't like; bedtime became a drawn-out endurance test taking two hours. Efforts to appease them were futile. We found we were constantly defending ourselves, arguing, fighting a losing battle over the

UPPER HEADROW 1930
The vacant site which eventually sold for £160,770 awaits the building of Lewis's store.

latest cause for complaint. Everything bought for the twins had to be exactly the same. Since no-one knew which object was whose, fights broke out as both twins claimed the same object. We tried to sidestep the problem by buying in different colours.

No go, useless. If one doll had red hair and the other yellow hair, both fought for the same doll. They'd chase each other screaming, hitting, scratching, biting. Soon the winner got tired of her prize, she'd look round and find the loser consoling herself with the rejected doll. Then all hell broke loose. The fact that one twin preferred X was enough to make the other prefer it too. The scrap was resumed at full blast. So no doubt you're thinking: Stop giving them dolls.

It wasn't only dolls. It spread to everything. They'd quarrel over two slices of bread and butter, alleging one was bigger than the other.

Eventually we checked that everything was exactly the same. This merely shifted the battleground. Very soon a toy would get scratched or broken, a dress stained or torn. Then both demanded the undamaged article, and whichever twin grabbed it made little difference. The loser would hurl abuse at Mam, becoming steadily more hysterical, always ending, "You don't love me!"

Her response was always the same, "Of course I love you. I love all of you." The way she said it wasn't convincing. Then, a short half-laugh that wasn't a laugh, "I couldn't send you back to where you came from, could I?"

This pretend question made everyone frustrated and furious. She seemed to be admitting their accusations by sidestepping an honest answer. It was significant that Betty and I never bothered to try the "you don't love me" routine, and the twins never tried anything else. It was a winner.

Steadily she let them have more of their own way; she stopped trying to control them. Then once, at the height of an argument with Dad, half-insane with fury, she blurted out the horrible truth.

When she was in hospital for that self-induced abortion, they'd shown her the dead foetus, the unborn baby she had killed. It was a boy.

I think something broke inside her. I understand the force of that question now.

"I couldn't send you back to where you came from, could I?" She would have sent them back to where they came from gladly, if she could have given birth to a boy.

I have known about this for many years. Until now it never crossed my mind to wonder about that unborn brother of mine - except to be glad he wasn't born. Only recently have I asked myself, what would he have been like? These tears I'm crying are the first I have shed for him. And they are not caused by him, though they are grief for him. It's just life.

Mam, I am sorry that I didn't leave school and get a job and bring home money to support myself - and you wouldn't have needed to abort your baby.

But I could not do any different. If it happened again, knowing what I do, I could not change myself. And if some force outside myself had made me leave school and get married, the outcome would have been a worse tragedy for me, perhaps for all of us. I know now, and knew then, my own nature. I can't live with second best. I'm glad I went to Oxford.

Red Silk Hood

During the war, as I grew up, I waged my own private wars. One was against school, the other against my father, but at school enemies were few.

There was only one real bitch on the staff, her name was Miss Vardon and she taught Domestic Science; a fancy name for cooking and cleaning. For this you had to wear a special white overall and learn first of all how to scrub down the plain deal tables in the DS room. It was not a subject that held me. Table scrubbing was all I learnt from her because Mam refused to give me any of the family's rations to "waste" on cookery lessons.

Still intent on building up Betty, Mam had refused to part with her precious eggs and marge, let alone dried fruit and sugar. So every cookery lesson I got a detention for not bringing the required ingredients. I couldn't cook; I hung around and watched the others cooking. I still can't cook.

Detention was three times a week and I scored five or six on average, thus making it impossible for me to serve all of them. After my first year and the transfer to "A" stream, I went wild. I was sent to the Headmistress for pretending to be a Flying Fortress in the gym and for pretending to be a tank in the library. My form mistress, a darling woman who tried to understand me, talked to me for hours and got a full recount of the goings-on at 8 Hares Terrace. There was nothing she could do about it but I loved all the attention she gave me, and was happy to prattle on about the twins and Betty. I grew bolder by the hour and at length was fool enough to boast, "There's nothing you can do to control me. There are only three detentions a week, and if I get half a dozen, I can do what I like."

She looked at me coolly.

"Gloria, you are absolutely right."

I beamed. I knew it!

"And because we know that you're right, we held a staff meeting about you, and decided that next time you cause trouble you'll be suspended. And if that doesn't work, you'll be expelled."

I was astonished. I believed her, too. She had that look about her that people have when they know they've just made a winning move. And she had won. Nothing changed at 8 Hares Terrace, everything was still as impossible as before, but my behaviour at school was modified so I was safe from expulsion. That taught me a lot about understanding children. You can't, really. All you can do is discourage them from running wild by making it not worthwhile.

I had another enemy on the staff, no bitch but a brilliant woman. Scottish and widowed, she taught French and was not fooled by my careful one-sentence-at-a-time copying. She was annoyed and relentless because she'd cottoned on to the fact that I was not learning my irregular verbs, not doing my homework, not revising for tests. Most other teachers resigned themselves to my inertia in class just as I had resigned myself to detentions, but she refused to give up. She had enormous energy and she taunted me constantly. In her lessons there was no hope of quietly reading a novel or doing somebody else's homework. She was at me all the time, pointing out I was intelligent but didn't use my brain, asking questions I couldn't answer.

The whole class was fascinated by Mrs Monkhouse because she was so much more alive than the other teachers and her moods were unpredictable. One day she'd come in to give a test, but she could be distracted easily by a question artlessly put - I was good at asking artless questions - and we'd spend the rest of the lesson hearing about France and her adventures, the test forgotten. At other times she'd launch a bitter attack on me. Bitter - she could be vitriolic. In spite of myself I'd flush up with fury, but I sat there smiling on the front row straight in front of her, a moronic grin on my face, learnt from William books. One day I was so hurt and furious that I realised there was only one thing to do. Teach her a lesson!

She had called me stupid. I did not relish being called stupid by an intelligent woman so the week before the exams I spent three whole nights studying French. I really learned all the stuff she'd been teaching throughout the entire year. In those days I had a perfect memory. Then I did the exam and made sure I came top by a margin so wide that cheating was out of the question.

I was looking forward to the sight of her face when she came in with the exam results...and taken aback when she announced that I had come first. Then after a pause she apologised, actually apologised, for calling me stupid.

I'd thought she would be embarrassed. That she would apologise never occurred to me. Of course she wasn't embarrassed, she had achieved the object of her exercise. We were friends from that moment on, I loved her.

Mam came up to school on two occasions only. One Open Day she arrived to complain to Mrs Monkhouse that instead of helping her with the housework, I read books all the time.

Mrs Monkhouse responded instantly, "Mrs Benjamin, you must be patient. Try to understand that Gloria's mind is busy with higher things."

Boy, did I treasure that statement. I thought it was the funniest remark I'd ever heard. Every time Mam asked me to do some housework, I'd yell back, "Try to understand that Gloria's mind is busy with higher things!"

The second and final occasion Mam went to Allerton was on my last Speech Day, to see me collect my Higher School Certificate, Leeds City Scholarship and State Scholarship. Without Mrs Monkhouse needling me I'd never have done it. For a State Scholarship which paid the best grant of all, you had to have *two* subjects at Distinction level. One of mine was English, the other French.

My History teacher, Miss Lees, small and old and very wise, was responsible for an equally important development. First, she taught us all about the French Revolution - not the conventional nonsense about Marie Antoinette and "Let them eat cake", but the economic and political causes.

We did the causes of the French Revolution in such detail that I was immune to anti-revolutionary propaganda for a lifetime. Then we went through the Revolution and its aftermath, and guess what? Even after Napoleon and the wars with Europe, the French ended up better off than when they'd started. So said my textbooks.

The next year she tackled Britain and our very own Industrial Revolution. She listed twenty-two possible subjects and let each girl in the class choose which she wanted to do. Thus, the Industrial Revolution in the Potteries, Shipbuilding, Railways, Canals, Cotton Mills, Coal Mining, Agriculture, Road Building, Education, Emancipation, and so on. I couldn't stop once I'd started. I found books in the Reference Library with such horrific details about working class conditions that I was left forever sceptical of anything an employer claimed. Child chimney-sweeps, children and women working fourteen hours a day on their hands and knees in the three-foot high seams of the coalmines. Employers constantly protested that their workers were well-paid and they could not afford to pay them better, even when five-year-old children fell asleep at the looms, fell into the machinery and died.

Book by book I waded through the horrific details of working-class history in Britain, ending up with a tome of two thousand pages - *Socialism in the USSR* by Sydney and Beatrice Webb. The picture of life in the USSR was so appealing in contrast to the Czarist past that I went out looking for the Communist Party. "Don't

call us, we'll call you," said the Leeds branch of the Party. "You're too young."

Well, I was thirteen. Only just, though.

Even in the Young Communist League, known as the YCL, I was the youngest of all. They met every Saturday night and held a social in rooms near City Square. So I became a Young Communist, much to Dad's disgust.

There were boys there, even men. In fact, the males outnumbered females by six to one, so I was perfectly happy. Russia was very popular when I was thirteen and Communism not the bugbear it became afterwards. I was quite ready to foment revolution theoretically and agreed that blood would run in the streets before the proletariat established its dictatorship in England's green and pleasant land. Meanwhile the revolution entailed only making scores of pilchard sandwiches and gallons of milky coffee. The war was over but rationing wasn't - it had got worse, and the country was poorer than before. The cheapest thing to put between two slices of bread was a pilchard, which festive fare was mine for years to come.

In the YCL we called each other "comrade" and believed it. We were all so young. I went to education classes in Marx and Lenin every week and read about the difference between a qualitative change and a quantitative change. Even today it still makes sense. The rest of Marx I took on trust and the works of Lenin bored me stiff, but I didn't miss a single class because the 'leader' was a miner called Robert Raymond Wilkinson. He had blue eyes with long black lashes and an incredibly clear, beautiful pink and white complexion.

There were three mining boys in the YCL and they all looked stunning. This was partly because of the coal dust. They were always cleaner than ordinary people because at the end of every shift they went to the pit-head baths to wash off the coal dust. And they always looked beautiful because the one place they could never get clean was the inside of their eyelids, where the dust lingered and produced the effect of Egyptian kohl. I thought Robert Raymond Wilkinson was lovely to look at, delightful to see and would be heaven to kiss. I filled an entire book of poems about my undying love, a collection of claptrap which sounded very good though it was mostly lies.

"Night after night I watched the stars with you," was a line from one of my efforts, in which I claimed to have been loved, deserted and left insomniac by RR Wilkinson. By the final verse I was weeping and waking night after night, watching the stars alone. In those days my poetry had nothing to do with reality.

SCHOFIELDS 1930

Older than Lewis's, Schofields' was more Yorkshire, more refined. Founded in 1902 its expansion was constrained by Cock and Bottle Inn. Full scale development followed the demolition of the Victoria Arcade in 1959.

The fact that I never shed a tear or lost a single night's sleep over him was irrelevant.

My communism was just as unreal as my poetry. Mam was onto me like a shot. She knew how much I hated any sort of change around the house, even much-needed objects to replace those glaringly old and labourmaking. When she had the old stone sink replaced by a normal modern sink, I was upset and furious. "What was wrong with the old one?" I demanded passionately. "There was nothing wrong with the old one! What do we need a new sink for? The old one was good enough! A sink is just for washing up and it was all right, the old sink..."

"Look at her," she'd say. "Ready to start a revolution, gerrout with yer! Wants to be at the barricades, God help me, did I give birth to an idiot! Gloria Benjamin the Communist of 8 Hares Terrace, can't stand it if her mother gets a new sink. You want to change the world, do you? God help the world, you can't even stand a new sink! Communist, gerrout!"

Dad treated my politics with a silent contempt which was far more withering. Withering but not effective. If he'd only talked to me and explained why he didn't trust Communism or any other ism, I could have learned from him, but this was the worst period in our relationship; mutual contempt flowed freely. We couldn't stand each other. We fought every night, often over the twins, often over money. The situation at home was the Second Front.

*

It is cheap and easy to laugh at the person I was, half child, half immature adult. The words I believed in and wanted to fight for were only slogans, but then, I believed in world revolution, equality, fraternity and socialism because I truly wanted the world to be a better place. I suppose I still do. Determined to save the world, it didn't take much to make me happy; a visit to a factory handing out leaflets at the gate, a Saturday afternoon spent selling *The Daily Worker*, evenings in full moon for painting slogans on walls - I had a wonderful time.

The tram journey into town was beautiful, though not as blissful as the journey home. To town and back, I travelled alone. Tramlines always fascinated me. Two shining silvery steel lines swept round curves or stretched away into infinity.

After rain the city streets were washed with gleaming water. The lights of street lamps had twinned reflections on the road, headlights of cars and the tram itself seemed to put pools of light everywhere. And the tramlines carried us on into the darkness, changing that darkness into light.

> *Once to every man and nation*
> *Comes the moment to decide*
> *In the strife 'twixt truth and falsehood*
> *For the good or evil side.*
> *...and the choice goes by for ever*
> *'twixt that darkness or that light.*

The tram would take me into town for an evening of adventure. Robert Raymond Wilkinson would be there, with his long eyelashes, a delicate intelligent face. Though I loved him he lived on the other side of Leeds and going home alone was the best part of the evening. Then I could sit at the top of the tram in the front seat, with the night black around me, gloating over every incident of the evening. Perhaps he'd accepted one of my pilchard sandwiches and a cup of coffee, or remarked with approval on the number of newspapers I'd sold. As the tram neared Harehills I'd go downstairs for my special bit of heaven. Getting off the tram was different from getting on. At the beginning you simply stepped on with the rest, but at the end, if you reached the step first, you could do something remarkable.

Just as the tram started to round a curve, I took a firm hold on the rails at each side and let my whole body swing out, held safe by my own grip. It was exhilarating to feel the strength of that grip, the cool night air on face and legs, the swing and throb of the night around me. My hair would stream out on the wind. I was a Valkyrie, I was a god riding the wind.

*

Though Mam and Dad disapproved of the YCL it never occurred to them that they should stop me from going. Maybe they hailed in relief an interest that was outside the world of books and included boys. Some of them were even Nice Yiddishe Boys, eminently suitable mates were it not for their crazy politics. There was Ronnie Blass and Sid Bloom, just out of the RAF and Sid, a chemist, no less.

Now whatever the rest of the Communist Party did about sex, I'll guarantee one thing: the Leeds branch of the YCL was respectability incorporated. While we were all revolutionaries at heart, the Party line was pure - very pure - Lenin. "Sex," said Lenin, "is like water, a necessity of life." He'd gone on to explain that you had to drink water, but clean water from a glass was infinitely better than dirty water from a puddle. Family life and clean thoughts were the order of the day, and besides I was the youngest girl in the YCL so everybody protected and lectured me. They'd never had a fourteen-year-old before and the last thing they needed was a nubile nymph distracting the lads from their revolutionary duties. Fourteen passed, fifteen arrived. I read more and more - the real damage was done by my books on psychology. At home the situation got worse when the war ended, Dad came home for good and the house filled with fights and miseries, beatings and bawlings, baitings and abuse.

Dad was the one I blamed but Betty and I knew that Mam caused the worst of it. She was systematically spoiling the twins. To Betty and I she seemed like a woman gone mad. They learned that they only had to scream - they were good screamers - to get anything they wanted. "You love her more than me," both of them would howl, taking it in turns to claim victim position. Betty and I teamed up, begging Mam to ignore them. "Why do you always argue and argue, then give in to them? Why can't you just ignore them?" we begged passionately. It was quite useless. She would argue at length against their most illogical assertions, statements never meant to be believed. Then she might hit them, but she always gave in afterwards. They were horrible to live with and horrible to watch at their game of tormenting Mother. I was safe because they claimed that they loved me.

Once I asked Mam for the thousandth time, "What are you doing this for? Why are you spoiling them silly? Don't you realise what you're doing?"

She gave me a very queer look.

"I know what I'm doing," she said.

"Then what are you doing it for?"

I'll always remember the rest of it.

"So they'll stay with me when I'm old."

I was speechless. She saw the incredulous look on my face.

"You'll leave home," she said. "You'll get your scholarship and go to Oxford. I know."

I could not answer. She was right. I dreamt of nothing else.

"And Betty will leave too."

I found my voice. "No, not Betty," I protested. For Betty was going to be good at cooking and gardening and all housewifely arts. Betty loved Mam and Dad in a softer way than I ever could.

"She doesn't know it yet, but she will. Betty will leave me and you'll leave me but the twins will stay with me. I know."

There was no budging her. After that day I didn't argue with her again. The trouble was she spoiled the twins and they tried the same tactics on Dad.

Dad wasn't one for arguing with them. He couldn't argue with such a load of rubbish. He'd laugh till they said something that made him angry, then he'd hit out. And once he started hitting, he hit hard and didn't stop easily.

*

In those years I think I despised Dad. He was nothing more than a brute in my eyes. I would even taunt him for being uneducated - I, who lived by his sweat. Can anyone on earth be as ignorant as a clever girl of fifteen?

I knew things out of books and next to nothing about reality. I was so ignorant that I did not know what I didn't know. It's hard to convey what I mean. Though I lived in the twentieth century and read Freud on Oedipus, for all practical purposes I might as well have been living in the Middle Ages; the electric light was as magical to me as ogres and fairy godmothers. I couldn't change a fuse or turn the gas off at the mains. Trams came and went and I rode on them, there was a boiler and water was heated, ships brought my food from abroad and a jolly good thing too.

I knew Dad worked hard - he was back in the cabinet-making - but as I had never strained my muscles and slogged away at a job until I could hardly stand, the fact that he worked hard wasn't real to me. It was pure theory. So he works hard, I thought, so what? Does that give him the right to come home and bully us and hit the twins and hit me? The hell with him.

Now I look back and marvel. Not at his brutality, at his forbearance. If I'd been in his place, there'd have been murder done.

I'm trying to find a way to tell the truth about myself. For example, I knew that the gas we used in the kitchen was made from coal and that coal was burned to produce gas in great coking-ovens. In 1947 I probably had a grasp of the chemical processes involved. But what I really knew was that I could turn the gas on and off and put coke on a fire.

Years later when I was teaching we took my class to see a great gas production plant that fed Leeds. It was like a scene from Hell. Huge conveyor belts were endlessly moving coal from the mines to the coking ovens. Every now and then the ovens would give up their coke and a gigantic, flaming mass of incandescent coal would topple into the waiting shovels; what noise, what stench! the fumes! the heat! We hadn't been warned about the heat. Standing on the roof of a factory our shoes were scorching - we had to move on, the soles of our shoes were almost burning. I remember thinking, "My God, no woman would ever have invented this. So this is what men do."

In that stench, that din, that heat, hundreds of men worked every day, so that I could have gas at my fingertips. They did not consider themselves heroes. What's more, the world in general didn't consider them heroes. An estate agent got more respect, more money and lived longer. But a worker should have respect from his own family, if not from the world, and our Dad deserved better than he got from me and the twins. For this I am still sorry. Betty was different; she gave him what he needed at the end of the day.

*

Remembering school, I remember many happy hours at Allerton High, spent belting out Christian hymns when I should have been in the Jewish girls' assembly. It was hard to be a Jewish girl because my upbringing had made me so weirdly un-Jewish. For example, Mam didn't know half the Jewish holidays and often sent me to school by mistake. Once arrived, I'd be promptly sent home. Of course she knew the great festivals such as the New Year and Yom Kippur, but the minor events such as Succoth and Shavuoth were beyond her ken. I hated missing school to stay at home baby-minding because of this superstitious flummery. The other Jewish girls deplored my ignorance; I was the low man on their totem pole. So throughout the years I skipped Jewish assembly as often as possible, and the only thing I got from the Jewish religion was the Sh'ma Yisra'el, which we said together every morning - "Hear O Israel, the Lord is our God, the Lord is One." I did not object to this as it made perfect sense, and went about as far as I was prepared to go.

My mother cooked a Christmas dinner every year and we teased her about it.

"You'd cook the right things for Moslem feast-days if you only knew what they were, that's how religious you are!"

She never denied it. "I would too," she agreed.

And on Christmas day we all sat round the table and listened to the King's speech, followed by Wilfred Pickles, like every other family in England.

The year I was fourteen, the war was over, pretty dresses back in the shops. My body was doing something quite interesting. For years, I'd been a fatty, but now rolls of puppy-fat started to disappear and I looked very fetching. Robert Wilkinson wasn't interested but there were others at the YCL who were. I had boyfriends - not particularly desirable boyfriends - but boy friends all the same. And then a man kissed me. He was an Irishman who silenced and awed me with a graphic account of what it's like to kill a pig. They scream blue murder. Then he kissed me and Dad's uniform beret, which I was wearing by accident, fell off. I was amazed. We had Reproduction of the Rabbit at school in Biology, with numerous diagrams. Miss Radcliffe who taught Biology was a lady of great refinement, and she'd assured us that Reproduction of the Rabbit was exactly the same for human beings. But when this Irishman kissed me, I knew she'd got it all wrong.

Sid Bloom was always hanging around hopefully. He adored me and was even ready to put up with the twins. So I was quite pleased with myself. The twins were determined to get rid of my boyfriends - their artless prattle with anyone I brought home began, "Are you going to marry our sister? We don't want you to marry Gloria." Sid refused to budge from Dad's armchair. One day they wrapped his RAF scarf round his neck and pulled from different ends. He simply disengaged himself. And though he was no part of my dreams and was completely unromantic, he kissed like an angel and sent the back of my neck into shivers - a feat nobody else has imitated before or since.

*

When I was fourteen the *Sunday Dispatch*, our Sunday newspaper, decided to run a short story competition. The prize was an incredible one thousand pounds

for the winner. There would also be a number of runner-up prizes of twenty-five pounds each, and all prizewinners would be published. At that time the *Sunday Dispatch* was immensely popular because it was a cross between *The News of the World* - Vicar confesses he interfered with twenty choirboys - and the snobbishly staid *Sunday Times*. Taking the *Dispatch* the Benjamin household got the best of both worlds.

I promptly sat down and typed a short story on the typewriter Dad had given me for my fourteenth birthday. The present had certain implications. He hoped I'd become so absorbed in typing that I'd leave school to become a secretary. A secretary could get paid for tripping off to work in an office from nine to five, with weekends off, and pay her parents for her keep and buy pretty clothes. Alas for them, pretty clothes came last on my list when I was fourteen. But my friend Matty had returned with her mother to Belgium at the war's end, and she wrote inviting me to come for a visit to Liege. Winning a prize could be the way for me to get the money.

My story was about the wife of an explorer. Patiently she waited at home for his return. Having explored everything else he was left with Everest. Well, it was there to be climbed. Our hero managed this and came home to cheering crowds and an adoring wife, who assumed he'd stay at home for ever now. With her. And they would live happily ever after.

There was one small snag. After their ecstatic reunion and dinner together, he wanders out onto the balcony and she finds him looking at the moon. That was the end of my story.

The story was published and I got my twenty-five pounds. By that time I'd reached fifteen and was hellbent on taking the prize money for my trip abroad. Mam was terribly hurt. It was the tradition in her family, in all Leeds Jewish families, to spend the first money you earned on a present for your mother. She'd done her bit, brought me up to an age where I was interesting to men and able to earn my own living, and she hadn't got her present. She wept with fury and disappointment.

In my defence: She hadn't told me what I was expected to do. Maybe she expected it to occur to me spontaneously? Well it didn't.

She would have stopped me if she could but something else happened; the story was syndicated and translated and sold all over the world. I got loads of fan-

THE JUNCTION OF HEADROW AND BRIGGATE 1940

The Headrow was remodelled in 1935. Unlike the Hippodrome and Lyceum - Greek words - Odeon is an acronym and stands for Oscar Deustchers Entertains Our Nation.

mail. Cheques kept coming in from other countries - I distinctly remember getting one from Finland. In the end I had enough money to buy Mam her present, get new clothes for myself and a return ticket to Liege in Belgium. Matty's mother even wrote to my parents assuring them that I'd be well looked after and they had no reason to disbelieve her. Neither had I.

*

My plans were for a holiday in Belgium, not a crazy adventure across Europe. What I didn't know about Matty was what she hadn't told me. What she was doing was illegal.

On returning to Belgium she'd become a Zionist, but in those days Israel did not exist. She belonged - and so did all her friends - to a secret organisation, the Haganah. They were busy training troops in the Ardennes, smuggling fighters out through Marseilles, getting them on illegal ships to Palestine. Once found within the three-mile limit off the shores of Palestine the British, then in control, fought to stop them landing.

The lucky ones sailed in at dead of night, disgorged their cargo on an empty coastline, to be picked up by equally illegal Haganah Jews and settled on kibbutzim. The unlucky ones were caught, arrested and interned on Cyprus. Some went straight from the death camps only to be put behind barbed wire again.

Her parents knew nothing about the Haganah link and the letter promising to look after me was quite sincere. They thought Matty belonged to a nice Jewish youth club!

While she was working for an underground organisation my only contact with Zionism was a little blue box with a white star of David on it.

At my grandparents' home it stood on the kitchen mantelpiece. At our home it stood on the living-room mantelpiece - and in every Jewish house in Britain and all over the world, the same little blue box with the same star of David had its place. Nobody ever bothered to tell us why it was there. Ignorance was the order of the day. Yet before the state of Israel existed, Israel was bought and paid for with the money in those little boxes. I found that out when I was twenty-seven and living in Jerusalem.

Every spare penny was put into the box, which had indecipherable Hebrew characters printed on it. Underneath the mysterious twisted letters was, even more mysteriously: *Keren Ha'Kayemet L'Israel*. It was in fact the Foundation Fund for Israel.

The box, the letters on it, the old man who came every Sunday to take out the money and write down the sum in a little black book - how was I to know what it was about? I never questioned it. I was completely incurious. Lots of men came to the house every week to collect money. The man from Pearl Insurance visited every house that the man from Prudential didn't. The business of getting yourself decently buried began with the first days of marriage; a man came "from the burial ground" for his weekly contribution. Then there was the chook man with his chooks and the landlord for the rent. We girls were polite to all of them, ignored all of them. The little old man was just a collector, almost invisible.

And slowly, slowly, the land in the Jezreel valley, a malarial swamp, was bought and paid for three times over. Not once. As the kibbutzniks said bitterly: Three times with money, and a fourth time with blood. First the land was bought from the sheikh who owned it, at his price. He might be satisfied, but his people were not. They would simply refuse to leave. So the land was bought a second time, and this time the Arab peasants got the price. They still wouldn't leave. A hefty bribe would be paid before they left, and this was just the beginning. The land had to be drained. Malaria was a killer in those days. But all that belongs to a different story.

What I want to explain was this: I had no desire to become a Zionist and no desire to leave England, which I knew was the most wonderful country in the world. Britannia ruled the world. In school we'd sung our way through *Merrie England* and no song was more precious to me than

> *O who are the yeomen, the yeomen of England?*
> *The free men are the yeomen, the free men of England!*
> *Stout were the blows they bore*
> *As they marched into war!*
> *Stouter their battle for the honour of England!*
> *And foemen to eastward and foemen to westward*
> *As bowmen did curse them, the yeomen of England!*
> *No other land could nurse them but their motherland, old England -*
> *And on her broad bosom did they ever thrive!*

I did not find this even slightly funny. I believed it.

So when I got ready for my wonderful holiday abroad, my last concern was the state of the Middle East. I worried about what was casually called the boat train. What exactly happened when you were on it - did it really chug onto a cross-Channel ferry? I was the first and only one of my family to go abroad willingly, as it were. My aunts and uncles marvelled and doubted. Abroad was wickedness, evil, sin.

Even without the Nazis, Europe was immoral and dangerous. And yet for three pounds ten shillings at Dover you could get on a ship which would carry you across the English Channel and when you got off at the other side you'd be in France! France, where the people spoke irregular verbs and subjunctives spontaneously, swigged wine as if it was water, ate real chocolate eclairs. I could hardly wait, though the train problem worried me.

On this, my first trip abroad, I carried a heavy suitcase. When the train reached Dover, everyone started to leave. How could this be? Didn't boat-trains go on boats? No sooner was I on the platform than a porter snatched my suitcase from me and gave me a number instead. I was absolutely terrified, convinced he was stealing my belongings. There was no way of getting the police to arrest him in this chaos - everyone was milling around wildly with suitcases. Even when my suitcase was restored to me on the ship, my faith in the porter's intentions wasn't. I had to tip him. Then I watched my suitcase like a cat with a mouse because everyone was a possible suitcase-thief. Why? Looking back, I think Mam and Dad must have overdone the warnings about Abroad.

We landed at Ostend where another porter, foreign this time, so even more likely to be criminal, grabbed my suitcase and disappeared for half an hour. I hadn't been sick on the boat because one of my ancestors had fought with Nelson on the *Victory*, therefore I couldn't be seasick. It was impossible. But I was damn near sick with anxiety getting through passport control and could hardly believe my luck - I thought it luck - when I ended up in a Belgian railway carriage, on the way to Brussels. When I reached Charleroi, all was well for about ten days.

Matty's stepfather didn't care what I did so long as I didn't bother him. Matty's mother was a lot less motherly than mine but perfectly normal as a hostess. The Belgian custom of shaking hands with everyone - family included - morning, noon and night struck me as amazing and they deemed me very badly brought up.

LEWIS'S 1949

When built the superstore cost over £750,000. Note the window full of nylons, the must-haves of the day.

Rudeness such as mine, not shaking hands with your mother, father, sisters, every time you left or entered the house, had not been encountered before. I thought they were simply crackers. They had cousins living a few doors down the street and this business of hand-shaking never stopped, no matter how often they popped in and out.

At breakfast you shook hands all round the table, just in case you'd lost the relationship in your sleep. It was my first encounter with culture shock.

However, Matty's cousins were a great compensation. There was a girl called Mariette and, more importantly, a boy called Gaby. He had golden hair and blue eyes and had survived the Nazi occupation because he looked so Aryan. He was lovely. I fell for him immediately and would willingly have shaken hands with him all day long. He returned the compliment and we went around holding hands mooning at each other. We searched deep into each other's eyes, sat together at picnics where he twined flowers into my hair, and sang together many songs he taught me. Very little else happened. We had not been instructed by TV or films that anything else was really necessary - left to ourselves, we might have reached the act of sex in a month or so, but we were never left to ourselves. Matty and Marie were not only jealous, they'd been warned by her mother to chaperone me.

I didn't mind. I was too happy to care.

Gabriel possessed a very rare quality; it would not be his for much longer, but he was seventeen when I met him, and he was totally happy. I don't know why or how. I have seen that quality of joy since, but only in young children. It existed in him as himself, not part of himself, and not dependent on any act or event. He was happy, and because he was happy, he sang. With the songs came a message: this was all temporary, it would not last, I was not to take him too seriously.

His favourite song was called *Sympathy*:

> *Ce n'est que sympathie -*
> *La sympathie profonde...*
> *Il faut, je le sais bien,*
> *Qu'on vous console, qu'on vous cajole...*
> *Mais si je vous prends à la main*
> *N'en faites pas un monde*
> *Ce n'est que sympathie - profonde.*

Well, I took the message with the song. Because he warned me so clearly, I certainly wasn't heartbroken when they told me the truth about their plans. They all belonged to a Jewish youth club, approved of by their parents. The youth club was not a youth club but a branch of the Haganah.

Their parents thought we were going to a kind of holiday camp in the Ardennes. I was going with them, of course, as Matty's guest. The holiday camp was in fact a training camp for the Haganah. We'd be trained to fight and shoot before being smuggled out of Belgium through France to Marseilles. Then we'd board an illegal ship to run the British blockade of Palestine.

I was frightened, I was furious. I didn't want to go to Palestine. I told Matty so. I had no intention of leaving England, my family, my life.

Matty pointed out that I could get back any way I liked, but I'd have to go with them or her parents would smell a rat; the whole group would be in danger if I defected. She made it clear that she despised me for not wanting to join the Haganah and fight for Israel; I made it equally clear that I thought she was barmy. But off we went to the camp in the Ardennes, hitchhiking to save the train fare. Gaby went with his sister Mariette. I was under Matty's wing. She lectured me sternly on the techniques of hitchhiking in Belgium.

"It's not like England. You'll have to learn to look after yourself. Here, put this in your belt. You'll have to learn to use it." It was a commando sheath knife. "Let them know you've got the knife, and if they start getting amorous, there's only one way out. It's disgusting but it never fails."

"Oh? What?"

"Blow your nose on your sleeve and talk politics. Especially Communist politics." She turned out to be absolutely right.

Within days of arriving in Belgium I was chattering away in my School Certificate French; Mrs Monkhouse would have been proud of me. So we made it to camp in one day, linked up with all the others, and there my troubles began.

*

Few girls could have been so utterly unsuited to become a member of an illegal terrorist organisation as I was. For although the Haganah only hit military and police installations, in those days it was terrorist enough. And Britain and British soldiers were the targets of every attack, for it was the British who were intent on keeping the Jews out of Palestine. The fact that I was British and proud of it did not make me flavour of the month at the camp; I soon learned that while I thought Britain totally blameless, the rest of Europe didn't. The parallel was sending a Catholic who believed in the Virgin birth to negotiate with a prostitute's collective.

Also, remember I was bookish by nature and lazy by inclination, with no talent for sports and especially no skill at aiming things - guns, grenades or arrows, all equally useless. Missiles were not remotely interesting to me. They tried to teach me judo and I refused to learn it. "But what will you do if you are alone in the desert with seven Arabs?" they asked. I am not making this up. They could seriously envisage such a situation. "I would never be such a fool as to get myself into the desert with any Arab," I retorted. They were as horrified by me as I was by them.

They practised fighting with sticks, fighting with rifles, hand grenades and sub-machine guns. The machine guns - old Czech rustiguts - were for the advanced class. I kept away, sneaked away, hid in tents, barns and forests. My participation was strictly confined to route marches and even so I refused to wear their youth group uniform, a sort of paramilitary shirt and shorts combo. They forced me to go on their damned route marches but I went dressed in a blouse and dirndl skirt, like a parrot in a school of crows. Wherever they put me in the column at the start, within ten minutes I mizzled to the end of it. Instead of marching along cheerfully I strolled slowly, swinging my skirt. They had to keep sending officers down to the tail-end to argue with me and make sure I didn't disappear entirely. It was exhausting for them and uncomfortable for me.

At first when they argued, I argued back. But then I realised I could never win any argument - there were too many of them, too emotionally involved in what they were fighting for. Within days I'd learned to look the officers in the eye and say helplessly, "Je ne vous comprends pas," in a thick Leeds accent. Matty and Mariette knew I was faking, but quite often an argument would arise over how much I was capable of understanding. I helped this along by looking stupid, and indeed my entire attitude was beyond their grasp. They were inclined to think I might be mentally retarded.

Once on one of these route marches, one of them dared to take a swig out of his water bottle before permission had been given. It was a very hot day, but the

VIEW ACROSS BRIGGATE LOOKING UP HEADROW 1928

This view is almost unrecognisable from what can be seen today. The building line to the right has been dramatically altered for road widening.

whole idea of the marches was to prepare us for desert warfare, so we had to get used to marching with minimum water. We had water-bottles, quite small ones, and haversacks and other objects to carry. The crime had been committed in full sight -one boy, one swig of water.

The punishment was in full sight too. He was ordered to empty his water bottle into the dust, every last drop of it. I flinched when I saw his eyes. There were hours of marching ahead, and he had no water. Worse, the whole troop shunned him; those who were water-greedy endangered the lives of others. No one questioned the justice of it.

I have more sympathy for them now than I had then. Underneath their bravado was desperation and misery.

This would emerge at night around the campfire. We'd be singing folk-songs, happily enough you might imagine, and then without a hint of warning, someone would double up in tears - jump up, run away from the camp fire, sobbing helplessly. Then two or three shapes would detach themselves from the circle round the fire and go to comfort their friend. So many of them had lost their families in the death camps that they had no grandmothers and grandfathers. There wasn't a single person there who had both parents living, like me.

"Lost" is the wrong word to use in connection with mass murder; it implies that by careless oversight on your part, your mother, father, brothers, sisters, aunts and uncles and friends disappeared into the distance. I felt their hurt and despair, but it had nothing to do with me, or so I thought. I just wanted to opt out of the whole mess.

As a sort of punishment for my un-military stance, I was set to digging latrines all day. Matty came to warn me that I'd better change my attitude or they'd make me clean latrines every day. "If Gaby and I hadn't spoken up for you, you'd be doing it already." Some holiday.

"They can't make me clean latrines if I don't want to!"

"Oh yes they can. They will. You'll see."

The truth was that I didn't have enough imagination to be frightened of them. Looking back today I can see horrific possibilities in the situation that I did not see then. And by good luck, I never had to find out how far they'd go to convert me to the cause of Zionism, because the next day a messenger arrived on motorbike from Charleroi. One of the group had split. Her parents knew. Within hours the police would arrive, raiding the camp. If Matty and her friends were ever to reach Palestine, they had to move at once. They did.

I kissed Matty goodbye, kissed Gaby goodbye, and waved farewell as they drove off on the backs of motorbikes. I might have wept a little, I don't remember. I had been given strict instructions by Matty to hitchhike back to Charleroi and say nothing to her family, just ride out their rage on discovering one daughter gone and two cousins missing, on their way to an illegal entry to a blockaded country. I imagined Matty's family in total hysterics, and I was quite correct. I had no intention of going back to Charleroi while everybody around me screamed, raved, wept and demanded to know where Matty and Gaby were.

I am amazed at myself now. Do you think I was worried at the turn events had taken, that they could all be killed, wounded or imprisoned? No, I was not. I was annoyed because they had ruined my holiday.

I'd arranged to spend a month longer abroad and I refused to go home three weeks early in disgrace. Somehow I had to salvage a holiday from those three weeks. I was in Europe and I'd only seen Belgium; I wanted to see Paris. I had a little money - not enough for a real holiday, but with hitchhiking and a diet of bread, cheese and cheap wine, I ought to be able to go home through France. I had a haversack with one blanket, a change of clothes and my passport.

My first idea was to hitchhike to the nearest town, Liege. A handsome driver who claimed to be a smuggler across the Franco-Belgian border gave me my first lift, and in Liege I wandered around seeing the sights. I recalled a certain parent who had visited the camp and spent a pleasant hour chatting to me. He'd given me his card with his name and address on it, and urged me to stay with his family for a few days before returning to England.

Because he must have been at least forty years old, I did not class him as sexually active. He might just as well have been Methusalah in my book. Some of his hair was grey, so by deduction he might have been older than forty - perhaps even fifty? - no entrant in the seduction stakes. Also his manner had been so fatherly that I didn't doubt his intentions for a second.

I rang him up. He was delighted to see me and because, as he explained, his wife was on holiday away from home and people might not understand if I came to stay with him, he arranged for me to stay at a pretty little pension-cafe in town. An old Jewish couple kept the pension, which made the place automatically respectable in my eyes. Happily I moved myself and my haversack into a modest room with a single bed, with a promise that I was to enjoy a week's holiday in Liege - nothing more was mentioned.

What the old couple thought, or what he told them, I don't know. I was to have my meals with them and we chatted away quite happily. Through the day I was left to amuse myself and explore Liege. At night, as soon as he finished work, he would arrive to take me out for the evening. Then the fighting began. He was swarming all over me.

Oh the disillusion of it - for both of us! He'd thought he was getting a fifteen-year-old English virgin for the price of a week's holiday; I'd thought I was getting a week's holiday for nothing at all. I argued, wriggled, slapped, pushed and bit. Once I started to scream in real earnest. He was terrified. Whatever else he was, he was no rapist. He hadn't the nerve.

After three or four nights of futile fighting, he was angry enough to tell me to get out. "I will pay your bill and you'll have to leave first thing in the morning. I won't pay for anything else at all. You can explain yourself why you have to leave. Go back to Charleroi. I would have given you a good time, but you're too stupid to understand."

When he had gone, I sat on the edge of the bed and wept. But I was not weeping for the situation he'd left me in, which was no worse than the one he'd found me in. At that time Europe was in the middle of the Berlin airlift crisis, and it was feared that war between Russia and the US would break out at any moment. I was reading the newspapers and listening to the radio - I was always a gloom-and-doom addict on international affairs. I wept because for unfathomable reasons Russia was now supposed to be everybody's enemy and if the Americans started to drop atom-bombs we'd all become radioactive dust. And I'd never get home again to see Mam and Dad and Betty and the twins. I'd die without even the chance of saying goodbye.

The old couple noticed I'd been crying at breakfast and asked me what was the matter. I told them the whole story in graphic detail. They were amazed, appalled, satisfied - it made a good story - and delighted.

"The rotten lecher," they said - or words to that effect. "We thought he was up to no good but we couldn't be sure. The sod! And you only fifteen! Don't worry about your holiday. You're going to stay with us for another week. "It's just a present from us. Don't think all Belgians are as bad as he is. Some of us are good people, decent people. You enjoy yourself for a week!" So I did.

They even sent telegrams to Matty's mother explaining where I was and promising I'd be back in Charleroi a week later. What nobody thought of doing, including me, was letting Mam and Dad know where I was. For three weeks I disappeared from the face of the earth and they suffered torments. I didn't write because I didn't know what on earth I could say. The truth seemed too bizarre to be believable. "Dear Mam and Dad. I hope you are well. I am well too. Matty took me to this Haganah camp in the Ardennes and then disappeared with a machine-gun on the back of a motorbike..."

It was during this week at Liege that I discovered my new power over men. I started to play a game. I'd go into a cafe, order a coffee and look around. Then I'd pick out the handsomest man in the place and stare at him. The game was to time how long it took to get him. Within three minutes usually he'd be on his feet heading for my table. Ah, those were the days!

When I finally returned to Charleroi I was met by Matty's mother, who was coldly furious. However, the ten days that had elapsed since Matty's group took off for Marseilles had done their job of calming everyone down. Matty had written explaining what happened and asking them not to blame me - they didn't exactly, but see their position: they were left with one girl, not their property, whom they didn't want, instead of another girl, whom they did. Mme Strassman wasted no time in getting my dirty clothes washed and my suitcase packed. She escorted me onto the train to Brussels herself, but of course she did not go with me, and that meant I was free. Free!

How could I not see Paris?

I bought a map which told me Paris was only 350 kilometres from Brussels. I could get there in one day's hitching, sleep at youth hostels and gradually work my way to the coast, returning to England not one week early with my tail between my legs like a beaten dog, but bang on schedule. At Brussels I started hitchhiking. My choice of take-off was inspired - just outside the local police station. Two policemen came out to argue with me.

They meant well. Together they scolded, admonished, depicted the dangers ahead. They managed to convince me that what I was planning to do was exceedingly dangerous and stupid. Did this make me change my plans? Yes, but

not in the way they intended. Looking back I can only state that the brains of all teenagers must be composed in equal parts of cotton-wool and glue; only glue could account for the sticking power of certain ideas. The cotton wool is there to act as a buffer between those ideas and reality.

Since I knew hitching to Paris was dangerous and stupid, I decided that if I arrived there safe and sound I'd go directly to Nôtre Dame Cathedral and light a candle to the Virgin Mary. This was the only alteration to my plans. And please note that I didn't believe in the Virgin Mary and I thought lighting candles was a quaint, beautiful but fairly primitive custom. My only knowledge of Notre Dame was seeing Charles Laughton as the Hunchback swinging from the belfry, completely bats. Even I was not daft enough to believe that the Virgin Mary, if she existed, would make a little note to protect me from all dangers until I got home. Yet this resolution had the power to comfort me, and when I reached Paris at five in the morning, I was determined to keep my promise. The lorry driver I'd been with put me down somewhere near Notre Dame, but I had no idea of where to go. The streets were empty, washed with rain after a sharp shower. I waited at a corner till I spotted another human being, a workman wearing the French beret and riding a bike. Dangling from his handlebars was a net bag and in the net bag were a dozen oranges. I stopped him and asked the way.

For half an hour this angel with oranges led me through empty streets, turning here and there, taking side alleys. He could have led me anywhere, he took me straight to Notre Dame. I kissed him farewell in gratitude, and he gave me six of his oranges. I have been given other gifts in this life but those six oranges, huge golden Jaffas, meant more to me than most. I went inside the Cathedral, bought and lit my candle, fell to my knees and prayed. I had plenty to pray about.

I stayed for a few days in Paris, but can't remember anything of note. From Paris I took the Nord 1 route, the equivalent of England's M1, the famous road from Paris to Calais, where the Channel crossing is shortest and cheapest. My first stop was at Amiens, where I found the cathedral and lit another candle - well, why not? Later, trudging around Amiens, I came across a museum. I'd been taken to the Zoo but never to a museum. No-one I knew had ever gone inside a museum. We knew what they were there for, of course, the same way we knew what the pyramids were for. People, living human beings, didn't go inside them. People went inside pubs, shops, hospitals, parks but not museums or art galleries. Well, my feet hurt

THE MARKET HALL 1940

Anyone looking above the first floor level sees just how beautiful Vicar Lane must have looked in the first decade of this century. By the 1940s it had become soot polluted, squalid. It took a lot of cleaning up to show just how interesting the 1904 Market Buildings really were.

and I wanted to sit down, and I remembered my art teacher saying, "Gloria, you can't afford to neglect any of the arts." So I went inside.

It was a revelation. I liked museums. From that day on, when I reached a new town, I went looking for its museum. There are lovely things in museums, as I was the first in my family to discover.

My last night in France was my worst. I got stranded as night was falling about fifty kilometres from the coast and I had to sleep in a field. There were scuffling noises all around me and I spent all night deep in statistics, calculating the number of French sex maniacs to the square mile. Come on, I said to myself, what are the chances that in this particular square mile of field you've got a sex maniac? Surely they must be a million to one against? Yet the terrifying scuttling noises went on and it was dawn before it dawned on me - simultaneously - that rabbits to the square mile come more frequent than sex maniacs and also make scuffling noises.

I reached England virginity intact, a seasoned traveller, used to having baggage snatched by mad porters, knowing that the boat train doesn't go onto the boat, able to order un vin blanc in a French cafe without attracting stares at my accent. Luck had been with me all the way. During those three weeks I hadn't written home, the body of a girl hitchhiker, dressed in green, my favourite colour, had been found in northern France and was still unidentified. Mam and Dad had gone through hell.

*

When I settled back in Leeds again, one of my fan-mail letters was so literary and admiring that I replied, and after corresponding, we took the chance of being mutually disappointed and met in City Square. I was wearing a brown hat with a dramatic brim that I fancied made me look at least twenty. And so I met Richard Stephenson Appleton.

Years later I kept coming across a poem of his published in just about every anthology in Britain, a poem about the atom bomb. "You have four minutes to get to your shelters," or something like that.

Back then he wasn't an internationally known poet but a reporter for the *Otley and Ilkley Express.* As a junior he had to review all the potty little amateur plays that were produced in draughty church halls around the West Riding - and he didn't have a car. We kissed in shop fronts and on damp buses travelling around Yorkshire. We sat on hard wooden seats and snogged in the back row, taking time out to watch bits of *Charley's Aunt*, *Arsenic and Old Lace*, *The Ghost Train* and *Hobson's Choice*.

Peter Appleton was an expert at French kissing, which I detested, and he had a lively line in seduction. "Gather ye rosebuds while ye may," he urged, hinting that I'd be an old hag within a year or two. "Then come kiss me, sweet and twenty, youth's a stuff will not endure." The time was *Now*, according to him. He was like Doctor Seuss arguing with Marvin K Mooney: "The time has come - the time is now."

Although the Berlin airlift crisis was over, we were all pretty miserable about our chances of survival in a cold war world and sure we'd be finished off by nuclear war before we could draw our old age pensions. It hardly seemed worth while to wait for anything, let alone having sex. I couldn't rebut his arguments because they seemed superior, but I still refused to have sex with him; I didn't love him. "That doesn't matter," he assured me.

But he wasn't even physically attractive to me. Every woman will know what I mean. There was nothing wrong with him, he wasn't ugly or repulsive, he was presentable and likeable - even handsome if you liked that sort of face. I didn't. Among his other advantages which he relied on heavily was that he'd been abroad too, a proper holiday in Switzerland, a whole fortnight. This made him cosmopolitan in Otley and Ilkley. He talked by the hour about Lake Lugano and Mont Blanc, finally making me the offer he thought I'd been waiting for. I could be his mistress in a beautiful Swiss hotel, he'd pay for it all, and give me the sexual experience I needed so badly. One passionate fortnight: the thrills and ecstasy of Appletonian ardour, and I'd come back to Leeds knowing it all. It would be like having DH Lawrence on the cheap.

He incited me with the wrong desire. I wanted to see mountains and lakes and Switzerland, in that order. When I rejected the offer he broke off the relationship; wisely, because I was still only sixteen.

Back in the forties there was a popular idea that once you had sex with anyone, you were hooked for good. It was considered as addictive as heroin. One session between the blankets and you ended up a sex slave, crawling at a man's feet. You wouldn't be able to live without it - you'd be utterly at his mercy.

This myth was reinforced by Adam's mother's pornography. The books in her house had spelled it out for me clearly. Now I realise that if a prostitute wants to keep her customers entertained, there's nothing like selling them the delusion that she's gasping for their favours. In those days I didn't.

Furthermore, the letters to the women's magazines confirmed the theory that once a woman "surrendered", he wanted no more of her, but she became almost insatiable.

All this was not encouraging news.

Like all teenagers, I was immensely curious about sex and wanted to find out exactly what I was missing, but not at the cost of becoming a blithering idiot begging for more.

So if you find my recital of all the men I fought off either boring or unbelievable or both, just remember I was young in my world, almost fifty years ago, no abortion on demand, no single mother's pension. What I wanted to do was go to Oxford and write great novels, not writhe around some man begging for a good screw. Perhaps at the age of six when Betty came along I'd experienced being shoved aside for somebody else - this was another reason why I valued independence so highly. Many women didn't.

The Sheikh was immensely popular and Rudolph made a mint by striding around with a horse whip looking sulky. There must have been plenty of girls hoping for the opportunity to be raped into submission, but when I said "no," I did not mean "maybe".

*

The summer I was sixteen the YCL held an International Youth Camp at some beauty spot in Yorkshire. By International they meant that people came from as far away as Manchester. It was there I learned to swim, and my heart was broken. Poetic licence. A girl called Nancy White with a tanned face and flashing, gleaming white teeth turned up; she was a real revolutionary as she worked in a factory. Robert Raymond Wilkinson fell for her and fell thumpishly. They were a true courting couple, mooning all over the place. I wrote some very dramatic lies about how much I was suffering and read a book of my absolutely dreadful poems to a tent full of girls. So powerful was my rendering of this rubbish that they were

BRIGGATE

Briggate led from Headrow down the bridge across the Aire. The street enters world history in 1888 when the inventor Louis Le Prince took the world's first moving pictures of some carts crossing the river from an upstairs window.

reduced to sobs and sniffles; I had to dash out into the bushes, pretending to be overcome with sorrow. Outside I got the giggles and couldn't stop.

The queer thing was that I didn't see the funny side of the situation until I saw them all in tears. I hadn't started out trying to con them. As usual, my awful poetry had been written in a mood of sincerity - it was only when other people started to take it seriously, that I stopped. Back in Leeds after the camp, Nancy White appeared to be forgotten; Manchester might have been a million miles away. I still went out selling *Challenge* and *The Daily Worker* every Saturday afternoon in the more depressing slums of Leeds. This meant I created a crazy, sub-criminal financial mess for myself as in order to please the comrades, I faked the number of copies I sold. Our house filled up with back copies of *Challenge* and *The Daily Worker* I paid for myself. This took all my pocket money; I didn't mind that, but eventually, as I sold fewer and fewer, I got into debt. I paid for the "literature" as the Party called it, but no-one paid me.

Now I could have sold many more of these dreadful papers than I did. People were very kind to young girls door-knocking in the slums, and with any enthusiasm I could have talked at least a dozen more customers into taking my wares every week. But I read *Challenge* and *The Daily Worker*, and they were boring. Boring, boring. No news, not real news, no interesting articles. Sometimes I looked glumly at the latest copy of *Challenge* and knew I could have written the whole thing better myself - unaided. The real challenge lay in selling the rotten things; reading them was demoralising. This was not the language of the *Oxford Book of English Verse*. It didn't occur to me that come the revolution all newspapers would be as inspiring as these two.

Nevertheless it hurt to take threepence from a worker in the slums who obviously couldn't afford it, knowing all he'd get was fish-and-chip wrapping. So I didn't. The day came when my literature bill ran up to three pounds.

Not much of a sum now, then a woman's weekly wage, but a fortune to me. There was only one place I could get the money from. My own bank book. My Yorkshire Penny Bank Book.

I'd been stashing away my pocket money ever since I got pocket-money. I don't mean the cash which came to me on a Saturday afternoon as soon as Dad got home from the Sheepscar Working Men's Club. The money I'm referring to now was in a class of its own, donated by aunts and uncles and you were not supposed to spend it. No, never! Never, ever! Why should you, it was silver, copper you could spend. Every Monday morning at Cowper St School you lined up with the rest of the class and put in your sixpence. There was even a Yorkshire Penny Bank service at Allerton. Nobody had ever been known to take this money out!

Putting it in was a sacred rite. Taking it out was - revolutionary? - no, worse, because revolution had already been imagined and carried out. Whereas I got the idea of taking my own money out of my bank book by myself. I needed three pounds desperately. Only desperation could have forced me to take such a step. I couldn't have felt more criminal if I'd plotted to rob the Bank of England. God, I was guilty.

I smuggled the bank book out of the house, drew out the three pounds marvelling at my own daring. Then I paid off the comrade who supplied the literature and told him the truth about my sales figures. I was no longer available to sell - or rather not sell - Party literature of any kind. But I remained in the YCL, though I wasn't the flavour of the month.

The YCL committee were amazed and furious. Sid Bloom took it all philosophically. Not so Robert Raymond Wilkinson, he could hardly bring himself to look at me. I sidled up to him and asked tremulously, "Bob, are you very mad at me?"

His answer was brief, "Yes I am."

That was the end of the conversation. I was really upset; it was about the last thing he said to me and shortly afterwards he became officially engaged to Nancy White. Glass of clean pure water all right, she was.

Unfortunately the evidence of my bank robbery remained in my bank book, in the shape of a withdrawal for three pounds. Mam was going through the wardrobe one day soon after and looked at the book, saw the withdrawal and called me to come. I confessed the truth.

The measure of how great my crime was became clear when she said, "I daren't tell your father. He must never know. He'd kill you."

I was really impressed. Normally she'd have rushed to break the bad news. But she kept her promise and Dad never did know.

*

We were studying Wordsworth at school and I became an addict. I soaked my brain in him. It was so full of Wordsworth that his poems came into my head constantly during the day. To me at seventeen Wordsworth was much like the Beatles were to a whole generation: *Penny Lane was in my ears and in my eyes.*

I didn't have a watch in those days. I didn't need one till I was thirty or older. By experiment I discovered that if I recited slowly *Ode on the Intimations of Immortality* from *Recollections of Early Childhood* it took ten minutes. The Ode became a convenient form of measurement, especially since it spoke itself in my head whether I was measuring time or not. I didn't have much choice in the matter. People marvelled at the way I could learn poems and ads but the truth was that anything I read three times was unforgettable. Sitting in a tram or bus just staring around I'd see some dotty little verse and read it over and over, and land myself with a ditty that ended, "So don't forget this golden rule: There is no substitute for wool."

So, loving the poems of Wordsworth I had to go to the Lake District to live the poems I loved, and the only way of getting myself to lakes and mountains was to take a job there. I was delighted when the Communist Party decided to hold a summer camp just above Keswick and Lake Windermere, and applied for a job as a kitchen hand. Ten shillings a week pocket money and all found - the "all" being a bunk under canvas. Off I went on the bus to Kendall, slimmer than ever before, prettier as never before, full of the joy of life.

Now there's not much to be said for working as a kitchen-hand, even in the Lake District, even though the Lake District was more beautiful than all Wordsworth's poems put together. In the mornings we'd look down on the lake and it was a mass of foamy white clouds; in the evenings at sunset whole mountain ranges turned translucent and stood like creations from fairyland, ethereal and glowing with a strange light from reflected sunsets.

Once, after a storm, we were called out of the kitchen tent: "Look! Look!"

It was a double rainbow, stretching from range to range, and the whole camp stood there transfixed. We wept. The tears streamed down our cheeks and no one said anything, and we stood silent amid the guy-ropes until the twin rainbows faded away. No one spoke of the scene afterwards.

COUNTY ARCADE

This was, and still is, the most elegant of the Leeds arcades. It was built in 1900 by the Leeds Estates Company at the turn of the century and originally contained 45 shops. Mnay of them were furniture and piano showrooms but there were also restaurants.

But after scenes like this I returned to kitchen tent, where there were boys. Lots of boys. Many more boys than girls, because boys were needed to take on heavier work - laundry and latrines and the cooking. Naturally I had to experiment with these boys. That's what flirtation is, a form of scientific curiosity. Flirting with boys became my pleasant preoccupation; it was mostly verbal, rarely physical, but dreadfully obvious to the adults who were running the camp. Not to me, perhaps - I don't think I knew I was flirting; I was having a good time. The fact that my good time was creating problems in the work force never occurred to me. If I got sent to the galley to collect a carving knife - they were always short of knives - all work in the galley stopped for twenty minutes. Wherever I went, work had a habit of stopping. When boys came to the kitchen tent to collect their sandwiches, they tended to stay around if I was there. One of them I liked very much. His name was Bob, and I had reason to believe he liked me too. In those days teenagers were more circuitous than they are now. If you liked a girl and she liked you, it wasn't immediately obvious that you should ask her out. You were surrounded by your comrades anyway. All sorts of delicate manoeuvres had to be performed. First of all, his group of boys invited me to go on a pub crawl with them. "You're wasting your time," I assured them, though flattered.

I'd been experimenting with alcohol too. Not beer, because girls didn't drink beer, but at weddings and Bar-Mitzvah's I'd downed gin and orange by the dozen. I liked drinks, especially sweet sticky drinks, and still do. I mean, Dutch cherry brandy and advocaat were my preferred form of alcohol, port and cream sherry and tokay came next. Good wine was wasted on me.

In those days I must have had a head of iron. Nothing seemed to affect me. I'd go on drinking but remain in charge of myself till I fell asleep. Once I downed twenty-four assorted short drinks but no one noticed any difference. "I might have been quieter than usual," I said, "but that was all." As I said to the assembled, "I don't get drunk."

"Never?"

"Never." I thought it only fair to add, "But I do fall asleep."

"You're lying. Come with us and we'll get you drunk." They were outraged. They were like people who cheat on their income tax facing an honest taxpayer. I was spoiling the game.

After much argument, we made a bet. I was to go with them on a mammoth pub-crawl through the streets of Keswick, and I was to drink all the gin and oranges they could pay for. Then they would test me on spelling and mental arithmetic and general knowledge, and if I got all the questions right I'd win five pounds.

Remember for years I'd been reading encyclopedias to fill in my spare moments. I was honestly concerned at the enormous loss of money they'd suffer - especially Bob. I knew they didn't have enough cash to get me drunk. I never became silly and giggly through alcohol, merely more determined to stay in charge of myself. So we set off one Saturday evening, walked the mile down to Keswick and visited pub after pub. Every time they ordered a half for themselves, they had to order a large gin and orange for me. By closing time I was still depressingly sober. I forget how many tots of gin I'd swallowed, but they began their testing programme on the way home. We were all walking uphill and I was alone; their questions weren't very taxing but though I was answering them correctly, something else was wrong.

The questions Bob was asking me were minor annoyances; all my concentration was needed to keep my body from dismantling itself. When he said at last, "You've won. We give in!" he slapped my lightly on the back.

I fell flat on my face.

We were all equally astonished. But my undignified collapse gave him the opportunity to help me to my feet and take my arm - Oh blessed comfort! - and let them all off the hook about paying the bet. Honour was satisfied.

After a time Bob and I carried on like a courting couple. We were not two adolescents having a flirtation; we were two lovers gripped by some strange forces of fate. We took to going off on long hikes together. The adults who ran the camp were terrified; I had to work all this out later - we were two innocents in fact, who kissed and talked and talked and kissed, and the adults were wasting their fears. In modern parlance, they were shit-scared that I would end up pregnant and besmirch the fair name of the Party. The comrades could foresee the headlines in *News of the World:* "Girl, seventeen, claims rape at Red camp" - "High jinks in Commie camp - girl gives birth to twins". That we were innocent didn't occur to them. We did lots of climbing because Bob liked climbing and one day we climbed a mountain nearby, and being utterly spent we fell asleep in each other's arms at the top.

Hours later when we woke up it was pitch black.

The next day there was hell to pay. Mercifully I've forgotten the details but Bob

was packed off back to Lancashire. He was older than me, he'd kept me out all night and this was a Bad Thing. The camp manager spoke to me very seriously, threatened to send me home pronto, cross-questioned me about what he suspected had gone on between us, refused at first to accept my version of the story and, no doubt from the purest of Communist principles, tried to find out exactly how sexually experienced I was. He was middle-aged and nasty. There was a scuffle in which he came off worst because he was unprepared for my behaviour. He got the message.

But he insisted that the flirting couldn't go on. If I was to stay to the end of the camp as arranged, I'd have to lay off the boys. Be a good little worker, a daily worker, or quit the Party forever.

The last four weeks of that camp were spent scrubbing tables. They only wanted me to wipe them down, but I was so miserable and furious that I scrubbed twenty long trestle tables every day, moving holidaymakers out of the way when they were chatting happily after an evening meal. I was bored too. I put on about a stone and a half in one month and as a consolation was presented by my mates with the collected works of Tennyson when I left.

Dad had come to pick me up at the bus-station and was flabbergasted at the sight of me. Luckily he didn't suspect I was pregnant, or if he did, he never let on. Gradually I returned to my normal size, permanently disillusioned about middle-aged men. Except Dad.

One day, going through the jacket pockets of his best suit in the hope of discovering a spare half-crown he'd forgotten, I came upon an inner pocket I'd not noticed before. It was just over his heart.

When I felt around, there was something in that pocket. Not money.

It was my photo. A clipping from the *Yorkshire Evening Post* article about me when I won the short story competition. That was all.

So I stopped stealing money from my parents at the age of seventeen.

*

No doubt about it, my last few months at school were idyllic. For once I studied seriously, well aware of my weaknesses - French and Latin grammar.

I got myself a huge French grammar book and worked through it from page one.

WOODHOUSE FEAST 1955

The Woodhouse Feast has a history going back to at least the early years of the nineteenth century. In the last few years major elements of the fair have relocated in the city centre outside the Art Gallery.

Having no illusions about my technical knowledge, I knew the worst hurdle would be the French scholarship essay, which I'd have to write in faultless French.

Sid Bloom's sister paid me five shillings a week to scrub her floors every Thursday, so I'd no need to beg pocket-money from Dad or steal it from Mam. Sid himself still hung around, always ready to take me to a political meeting or a YCL social, willing to argue for hours about the imminent revolution, and taking the prospect of my absence in Oxford as just one of those things. He wanted me to get educated.

I can't say the same for Mam and Dad, but let's try to understand them. Dad first: he had no son. Secondly, he had no money. Other Jews to right and left were scooping in the stuff. They had heads for business, Dad hadn't. He was a right bonny worker and he worked twelve, thirteen hours a day, but Mam hadn't had a holiday for fifteen years and we were still living in Harehills when all the successes were moving out to Roundhay and Moortown. Even Dad's partner was rich compared to Dad, because he had one daughter instead of four, and he didn't drink or smoke. Mam's family pitied her because she'd backed the wrong horse, so to speak.

However, there was one way in which Mam could recoup her fortunes in a single stroke. Grandsons. Even one would make her a winner. As a status symbol in our community, a six-pound baby boy would beat a Rolls-Royce. Even granddaughters were better than nothing. A woman could produce pictures of her granddaughters, worry about them, complain they weren't being brought up properly. She'd have a stake in the future.

All she needed was my co-operation.

But what use to her was an educated daughter? I had to get married and get pregnant - and what nice Yiddishe boy would want a wife with a university degree? Educated wives were no good - not unless they had money too, in which case the money might compensate, but only partly, for a bride who kept quoting Shakespeare and McDougall's *Abnormal Psychology*.

In 1950 Mam knew she'd never get a place in the grandmother stakes while her eldest daughter preferred books to babies.

ALLERTON GIRLS HIGH SCHOOL 1947

This school, opened by the Princess Royal, was built in 1939 when the earlier private school moved up from Chapel Allerton. Most of the girls were fee-paying but some, like Gloria, came in as scholarship girls.

*

As the scholarship exam drew closer, we both got nerves. The last week was sheer hell. I couldn't sleep for fright. All was riding on the three-hour French paper - I had no worries about the English. Now insomnia is not the worst thing that can happen, but it had never happened to me before and I was terrified. I'd always revelled in exams, but before I'd always slept like a log five minutes after jumping into bed. Now my body was behaving as if an alien was taking over. Horror, horror. So I rushed to a doctor who prescribed sleeping pills which he swore would leave my head clear for the exams.

How? If they were strong enough to put me to sleep, how could my brain be alert? I didn't believe him. I didn't dare take the pills.

All was lost. All... For I couldn't do the scholarship exam without a good night's sleep, and I couldn't get a good night's sleep without taking the pills, and if I took the pills I wouldn't be alert for the exam. Woe, alas, ruin!

The night before the dreaded French scholarship paper, Sid Bloom turned up after tea and announced he had come to take me to a YCL dance.

To a what?

A dance.

Did he realise I had a scholarship exam in the morning?

He did.

"And she hasn't slept a wink for three nights together!" Mam moaned.

Now Sid had black curly hair and round cherubic cheeks, like an ugly stunted angel without wings. But he was a highly trained debater, about the only person within a five-mile radius who could front up to Mam at her rhetorical best without twitching an eyelash. His debating technique was to listen to every word his opponent said with great concentration, and without interruption. Standing patiently by the door, he let Mam and me rave on until we'd exhausted ourselves. He had dropped his eyelids and was smiling a set, enigmatic half-smile that signified: all will be well.

When we both fell silent after hysterically assuring him that dancing was the last thing on my programme for the night, he asked politely what I intended to do instead?

"I shall go to bed at eight o'clock."

VICTORIA ARCADE CORONATION DECORATION 1953

The Victoria Arcade (1898), though marginally older than the stylish County Arcade (1903), was a central feature of the expanding retail trade of Leeds. These shopping malls replaced cramped inner city slums and were expressions of consumer spending. The Victoria Arcade was demolished in 1959 to make room for Schofields'.

"To do what?"

"To try to get some sleep!"

"But you know you won't be able to sleep," he pointed out nicely.

"I know that, but at least I'll be in bed!"

"Lying awake in bed?"

"Well, yes. What else can I do?"

"You can come dancing with me."

"But I'll lose the scholarship!"

"I'll bring you home early," Sid promised. "Then you can lie awake in bed and worry about the exam all night. A few hours' dancing won't make that much difference."

But it did. He brought me home at twelve-thirty in the morning and I had a wonderful time. We kissed goodnight at the garden gate. There was a full moon of amazing silver swimming overhead. "A perfect night," I sighed, cuddling into his arms.

"Perfect," he agreed. "On a night like this we could have been out painting slogans on walls."

Oh well, I thought, to hell with the scholarship.

That night I slept like a log, woke with my brain crystal clear and waltzed through the French scholarship examination.

I was offered two different scholarships; poor Dad was bemused at the weird transition from failure to success, Mam disappointed but resigned. She would transfer her efforts to Betty.

So I said goodbye to Leeds and childhood, little knowing they'd be always with me; silver tramlines in my brain stretching on to eternity, taking me home where I belong.